STYLE

The Basics of Clarity and Grace

Third Edition

Joseph M. Williams
The University of Chicago

PEARSON
Longman

New York San Francisco Boston
London Toronto Sydney Tokyo Singapore Madrid
Mexico City Munich Paris Cape Town Hong Kong Montreal

To my mother and father

Senior Sponsoring Editor: Virginia L. Blanford
Senior Marketing Manager: Sandra McGuire
Production Manager: Stacey Kulig
Project Coordination, Text Design, and Electronic Page Makeup: Pre-Press PMG
Senior Cover Design Manager: Nancy Danahy
Cover Designer: Nancy Sacks
Cover: ©Joel Zimmerman
Manufacturing Manager: Mary Fischer
Printer and Binder: Courier
Cover Printer: Coral Graphics Services

Library of Congress Cataloging-in-Publication Data

Williams, Joseph M.
   Style : the basics of clarity and grace / Joseph M. Williams.
      p. cm.
   Includes index.
   ISBN-13: 978-0-205-60535-4
   ISBN-10:   0-205-60535-4
   1. English language—Rhetoric. 2. English language—Technical
English. 3. English language—Business English. 4. English language—
Style. 5. Technical writing. 6. Business writing. I. Title.
PE1421.W5455 2008
808'.042--dc22

Library of Congress Control Number: 2007046105

Copyright © 2009 by Pearson Education, Inc.

Please visit us at www.ablongman.com

ISBN 13: 978-0-205-60535-4
ISBN 10:   0-205-60535-4

5 6 7 8 9 10—CRW—10 09

. . . English style, familiar but not coarse,
elegant, but not ostentatious . . .
—SAMUEL JOHNSON

Contents

Preface

Most people won't realize that writing is a craft.
You have to take your apprenticeship in it like anything else.
—KATHERINE ANNE PORTER

In this third edition of *Style: The Basics*, I've done a good deal of tightening up so that I could add new material in almost every lesson, but especially in lessons 2, 6, 7, and 8. In 8, I offer a general principle of style that I don't think has been stated before, and for entirely aesthetic reasons, I've rounded off all the lessons with epigrams that sum up their substance. But this third edition aims at answering the same questions I asked in the first and second:

- What is it in a sentence that makes readers judge it as they do?

- How can we diagnose our own prose to anticipate their judgments?

- How can we revise a sentence so that readers will think better of it?

The standard advice about writing ignores those questions. It is mostly truisms like "Make a plan" and "Think of your audience"—advice that most of us ignore as we wrestle ideas out onto the page. When I first drafted this paragraph, I wasn't thinking about you; I was struggling to get my own ideas straight. What I did know was that I would come back to this paragraph again and again, and that it was likely to be only then—as I revised—that I could think about you and discover the plan that fit my draft. I also knew that as I did so, there were some principles I could rely on. This book explains them.

Principles, Not Prescriptions

Those principles may seem prescriptive, but that's not how I intend them. I offer them as ways to help you predict how readers will judge your prose and then help you decide whether and how to revise it. As you learn all these principles, you may find that you write more slowly. That's inevitable. Whenever we reflect on what we do as we do it, we become self-conscious, sometimes to the point of paralysis. It passes. You can avoid some of that paralysis if you remember that these principles have little to do with how you draft, much to do with how you revise. If there is a first principle of drafting, it's to forget advice about how to do it.

To learn how to revise efficiently, though, you have to know a few things:

- You should know a few grammatical terms: subject, verb, noun, active, passive, clause, preposition, and coordination.
- You will have to learn new meanings for two familiar words: topic and stress.
- You will need five terms that you probably don't know. Two are important: nominalization and metadiscourse; three are useful: resumptive modifier, summative modifier, and free modifier.

Finally, if you are reading this book on your own, go slowly. It is not an amiable essay to read in a sitting or two. Take the lessons a few pages at a time, up to the exercises. Do the exercises, edit someone else's writing, then some of your own written a few weeks ago, then something you've written that day.

If you find these principles useful and would like a text that offers a fuller discussion of style as well as revision exercises, a longer version is available: *Style: Lessons in Clarity and Grace*, ninth edition. Order by using ISBN 0-321-47935-1.

ACKNOWLEDGMENTS

So many have offered support, suggestions, and criticisms over the last twenty-five years, that I cannot thank you all. I have learned from undergraduate, graduate, and professional students, and post-docs who have gone through the Little Red Schoolhouse writing program at the University of Chicago (a.k.a. Advanced Academic and Professional Writing). I am equally grateful to the graduate students who taught these principles and offered important feedback.

For several years, I have had the good fortune to work with two people who have been both good colleagues and good friends and whose careful thinking has helped me think better about many matters, both professional and personal: Don Freeman and Greg Colomb. Don's careful readings have saved me from more than a few howlers; I am indebted to him for the quote from William Blake in Lesson 8. For more than twenty-five years now, Greg has put up with more than most friends would, and I have benefited from both his scrupulous critical thinking and our intemperate shouting matches. It has been a pleasure and a privilege to work with him and to travel and hang out with him and Sandra.

And again, those who contribute more to my life than I let them know: In the first edition, there were six. Now, there are eighteen: Michele, Oliver, and Eleanor; Ingrid and Chris; Patty, Dave, Matilde, and Owen; Megan, Phil, Lily, and Calvin; Christine, Joe, Katherine, and Nicholas. And at beginning and end still, Joan, whose patience and love continue to flow more generously than I deserve.

J. M. W.

South Haven, Michigan

Understanding Style

*Have something to say,
and say it as clearly as you can.
That is the only secret of style.*
—MATTHEW ARNOLD

CLARITY AND UNDERSTANDING

This book rests on two principles: it is good to write clearly, and anyone can. The first is self-evident, especially to those who read a lot of writing like this:

> An understanding of the causal factors involved in excessive drinking by students could lead to their more effective treatment.

But that second principle may seem optimistic to those who can't get close to this:

> We could more effectively treat students who drink too much if we understood why they do.

Of course, writing fails for reasons more serious than unclear sentences. We bewilder readers when we can't organize complex ideas coherently. And they won't even read what we've written unless we motivate them to. But once we've formulated our claims, organized supporting reasons, grounded them on sound evidence, and motivated readers to read attentively, we must still express it all clearly, a difficult task for most writers and a daunting one for many.

It is a problem that has afflicted generations of writers who have hidden their ideas not only from their readers, but sometimes even from themselves. When we read that kind of writing in government regulations, we call it *bureaucratese;* in legal documents, *legalese;* in academic writing that inflates small ideas into gassy abstractions, *academese.* Written deliberately or carelessly, it is a language of exclusion that a democracy cannot tolerate.

THE IRRESISTIBLE LURE OF OBSCURITY

In the best-known essay on English style, "Politics and the English Language," George Orwell anatomized the turgid language of politicians, academics, and other such speakers and writers:

> The keynote [of a pretentious style] is the elimination of simple verbs. Instead of being a single word, such as *break, stop, spoil, mend, kill,* a verb becomes a phrase, made up of a noun or adjective tacked on to some general-purposes verb such as *prove, serve, form, play, render.* In addition, the passive voice is wherever possible used in preference to the active, and noun constructions are used instead of gerunds (*by examination* of instead of *by examining*).

But in abusing that style Orwell adopted it. He could have written more concisely:

> Pretentious writers avoid simple verbs. Instead of using one word, such as *break, stop, kill,* they turn the verb into a noun or adjective, then tack onto it a general-purpose verb such as *prove, serve, form, play, render.* They use the passive voice everywhere instead of the active, and noun constructions instead of gerunds (*by examination* instead of *by examining*).

If the best-known critic of a turgid style could not resist it, we shouldn't be surprised that politicians and academics embrace it. On the language of the social sciences:

> A turgid and polysyllabic prose does seem to prevail in the social sciences. . . . Such a lack of ready intelligibility, I believe, usually has little or nothing to do with the complexity of thought. It has to

do almost entirely with certain confusions of the academic writer about his own status.

> —C. Wright Mills, *The Sociological Imagination*

On the language of medicine:

> It now appears that obligatory obfuscation is a firm tradition within the medical profession. . . . [Medical writing] is a highly skilled, calculated attempt to confuse the reader. . . . A doctor feels he might get passed over for an assistant professorship because he wrote his papers too clearly—because he made his ideas seem too simple.

> Michael Crichton, *New England Journal of Medicine*

On the language of law:

> In law journals, in speeches, in classrooms and in courtrooms, lawyers and judges are beginning to worry about how often they have been misunderstood, and they are discovering that sometimes they can't even understand each other.

> —Tom Goldstein, *New York Times*

On the language of science:

> There are times when the more the authors explain [about ape communication], the less we understand. Apes certainly seem capable of using language to communicate. Whether scientists are remains doubtful.

> —Douglas Chadwick, *New York Times*

Most of us first confront that kind of writing in textbook sentences like this one:

> Recognition of the fact that systems [of grammar] differ from one language to another can serve as the basis for serious consideration of the problems confronting translators of the great works of world literature originally written in a language other than English.

In about half as many words, that means,

> When we recognize that languages have different grammars, we can consider the problems of those who translate great works of literature into English.

Generations of students have struggled with dense writing, many thinking they weren't smart enough to grasp a writer's deep ideas. Some have been right about that, but more could have blamed the writer's inability (or refusal) to write clearly. Many students, sad to say, give up; sadder still, others learn not only to read that style but write it, inflicting it in turn on their readers, thereby sustaining a 450-year-old tradition of unreadable writing.

SOME PRIVATE CAUSES OF UNCLEAR WRITING

Unclear writing is a social problem, but it often has private causes. Michael Crichton mentioned one: some writers plump up their prose to impress those who think that complicated sentences indicate deep thinking. And in fact, when we want to hide the fact that we don't know what we're talking about, we typically throw up a tangle of abstract words in long, complicated sentences.

Others write graceless prose not deliberately but because they are seized by the idea that writing is good only when it is free of errors that only a grammarian can explain. They approach a blank page not as a space to explore new ideas, but as a minefield to cross gingerly. They creep from word to word, concerned less with their readers' understanding than with their own survival. I address that issue in Lesson 2.

Others write unclearly because they freeze up, especially when they are learning to think and write in a new academic or professional setting. The afflicted include not just undergraduates taking their first course in economics or psychology, but graduate students, businesspeople, doctors, lawyers—anyone writing on a new topic for unfamiliar and therefore intimidating readers.

As we struggle to master new ideas, most of us write worse than we do when we write about things that we understand better. If that sounds like you, take heart: you will write more clearly when you more clearly understand what you are writing about.

But the biggest reason most of us write unclearly is that we don't know when we do, much less why. Our own writing seems clearer to us than it does to our readers, because we read into it what we want them to get out of it. And so instead of revising our writing to meet their needs, we send it off the moment it meets ours.

In all of this, of course, there is a great irony: we are likely to confuse others when we write about a subject that confuses us. But when we also read about a confusing subject written in a complex style, we too easily assume that its complexity signals deep thought, and so we try to imitate it, compounding our already-confused writing.

This book shows you how to avoid that trap, how to read your own writing as others will, and, when you should, how to improve it.

On Writing and Rewriting

A warning: If you think about these principles *as you draft*, you may never finish drafting anything. Most experienced writers get something down on paper or up on the screen as fast as they can. Then as they rewrite that first draft into something clearer, they understand their ideas better. And when they understand their ideas better, they express them more clearly, and the more clearly they express them, the better they understand them . . . and so it goes, until they run out of energy, interest, or time.

For a fortunate few, that moment comes weeks, months, even years after they begin. (Over the last twenty-five years, I've wrestled this book through dozens of drafts, and there are parts I still can't get right.) For most of us, though, the deadline is closer to tomorrow morning. And so we have to settle for prose that is less than perfect, but as good as we can make it. (Perfection is the ideal, but an obstacle to done.)

So use what you find here not as rules to impose on every sentence *as* you draft it, but as principles to help you identify sentences you've already written that might give your readers a problem, and then to analyze, and, if necessary, revise those sentences quickly.

As important as clarity is, though, some occasions call for more:

> Now the trumpet summons us again—not as a call to bear arms, though arms we need; not as a call to battle, though embattled we are; but a call to bear the burden of a long twilight struggle, year in and year out, "rejoicing in hope, patient in tribulation," a struggle against the common enemies of man: tyranny, poverty, disease and war itself.
>
> —John F. Kennedy, Inaugural Address, January 20, 1961

Few of us are called upon to write a presidential address, but in even our modest prose, some of us take a private pleasure in writing a shapely sentence, regardless of whether anyone notices. If you enjoy not just writing a sentence but crafting it, you will find suggestions in Lesson 9. Writing is also a social act that might or might not serve the best interests of your readers, so in Lesson 10, I address some issues about the ethics of style.

Many years ago, H. L. Mencken wrote this:

> With precious few exceptions, all the books on style in English are by writers quite unable to write. The subject, indeed, seems to exercise a special and dreadful fascination over school ma'ams, bucolic college professors, and other such pseudoliterates. . . . Their central aim, of course, is to reduce the whole thing to a series of simple rules—the overmastering passion of their melancholy order, at all times and everywhere.

Mencken was right: no one learns to write well by rule, especially those who cannot feel or think or see. But I know that many do see clearly, feel deeply, and think carefully but can't write sentences that make their thoughts, feelings, and visions clear to others. I also know that the more clearly we write, the more clearly we see and feel and think. Rules help no one do that, but some principles can. The first is to put your readers ahead of yourself:

> Essentially style resembles good manners. It comes of endeavouring to understand others, of thinking for them rather yourself—or thinking, that is, with the heart as well as the head.

> —Sir Arthur Quiller-Couch

2

Correctness

*No grammatical rules have sufficient authority to control the
firm and established usage of language. Established custom,
in speaking and writing, is the standard to which we must
at last resort for determining every controverted point in
language and style.*
—HUGH BLAIR

CORRECTNESS, OBEDIENCE, AND CHOICE

To a careful writer, nothing is more important than choice, but
in some matters, we have none—we can't put *the* after a noun,
as in *street the*. But we choose when we can. For example, if you
wanted readers to think you wrote clearly, which of these sentences would you choose to write?

1. Lack of newspaper media support was the cause of our
   election loss.
2. We lost the election because the media did not support us.

Most of us choose (2).

Unlike clarity, though, correctness seems a matter not of
choice, but of obedience. When the *American Heritage Dictionary*
says that *irregardless* is "never acceptable" (except, they say, for
humor), our freedom to choose it seems at best academic. In
matters of this kind, we choose not between better and worse,

but between right and utterly, irredeemably, unequivocally Wrong. Which, of course, is no choice at all.

But that lack of choice does seem to simplify things: "correctness" requires not sound judgment but only a good memory. If we remember that *irregardless* is always wrong, it ought not rise to an even subconscious level of choice. Some teachers and editors think we should memorize dozens of such "rules":

- Never begin a sentence with *and* or *but*.
- Never use double negatives.
- Never split infinitives.

Correctness, however, needs more than a good memory. Some rules are real: our verbs must agree with subjects; our pronouns must agree with their referents. If we ignore such rules, we risk being labeled at least unschooled. But a handful of other often repeated rules are less important than many think, and some are not real rules at all. If you obsess over them all, you hinder yourself from writing quickly and clearly. That's why I address "correctness" now, before clarity, because I want to put it where it belongs—behind us.

THREE KINDS OF RULES

Misguided opinions about correctness have been encouraged by generations of grammarians who, in their zeal to codify "good" English, have confused three kinds of "rules":

1. Some rules—call them the "Real Rules"—define what makes English English—articles precede nouns: *the book*, not *book the*.

   Speakers born into English don't think about these rules at all and violate them only when they are careless, distracted, or tired.

2. A few other rules—call them "the rules of *Standard* English"—distinguish the standard dialect from nonstandard

ones: *He doesn't have any money* versus *He don't have no money.*

Schooled writers follow these rules as naturally as they do the Real Rules and think about them only when they notice others violating them. The only writers who *self-consciously* follow them are those who were not born into Standard English and are striving to join the educated class.

3. Finally, some grammarians have invented a handful of rules that they think we all *should* observe—call them "Folklore."

These are the rules that many well-educated writers obsess over. Most date from the last half of the eighteenth century:

> Don't split infinitives, as in *to **quietly** leave.*
>
> Don't end a sentence with a preposition, as in *He is the one I spoke **to.***

A few date from the twentieth century:

> Don't use *hopefully* for *I hope,* as in ***Hopefully,** it won't rain.*
>
> Don't use *which* for *that,* as in *a car **which** I sold.*

For 250 years, grammarians have accused the best writers of violating these invented rules, and for 250 years those writers have ignored them. Which is lucky for the grammarians, because if we did obey all their rules, the grammarians would have to keep inventing new ones or find another line of work. The fact is, none of these invented rules reflects the consensus of unself-conscious usage of our best writers.

In this lesson, we focus on this third kind of rule, the handful of invented ones, because only they vex those who already write Standard English.

It is, however, no simple matter to deal with these rules if you want to be thought of as someone who writes "correctly." You could choose the worst-case policy: follow all the rules all the time because sometime, someone will criticize you for something—for beginning a sentence with *and* or ending it with *up*.

But if you mindlessly obey all the rules all the time, you risk becoming so obsessed with them that you tie yourself in knots. And sooner or later, you will impose those rules—real or not—on others. After all, what good is learning a rule if all you can do is obey it?

The alternative to blind obedience is selective observance. But then you have to decide which rules to observe and which to ignore. And if you ignore an alleged rule, you may have to deal with those whose passion (and memory) for "good" grammar seems to endow them with the moral authority to see in a split infinitive a sign of spiritual corruption and social decay.

If you want to avoid being accused of "lacking standards," but refuse to submit to whatever "rule" someone can dredge up from ninth-grade English, you have to know more about these invented rules than the rule-mongers do. The rest of this lesson helps you do that.

TWO KINDS OF INVENTED RULES

We can sort most of these invented rules into two groups: Folklore and Elegant Options.

1. *Folklore.* When you violate these "rules," few careful readers notice, much less care. So they are not rules at all, but folklore you can ignore (unless you are writing for someone with the power to impose these rules on you).

2. *Elegant Options.* When you ignore these rules, few readers notice. But paradoxically, some do when you observe them, because they think they detect in your writing signals of special care. So you can observe these rules or not, depending on how you want a few especially careful readers to respond.

Folklore

These rules include those that most careful readers and writers ignore. You may not yet have had some of them inflicted on you, but chances are that one day you will. In what follows, the quotations that illustrate "violations" are from writers of considerable intellectual and scholarly stature or who, on matters of usage, are reliable conservatives (some are both). A check mark indicates acceptable Standard English, despite the claims of some grammarians who mistakenly think otherwise.

1. **"Don't begin sentences with *and* or *but*."** This passage ignores the "rule" twice (my emphasis in all examples that follow):

   ✓ **But,** it will be asked, is tact not an individual gift, therefore highly variable in its choices? **And** if that is so, what guidance can a manual offer, other than that of its author's prejudices— mere impressionism?

   —Wilson Follett, *Modern American Usage: A Guide*,
   edited and completed by Jacques Barzun et al.

   On this matter, it is useful to consult the guide to usage most esteemed by conservative writers: the *second* edition of H. W. Fowler's *A Dictionary of Modern English Usage* (first edition, Oxford University Press, 1926; second edition, 1965; third edition, 1997, considered grammatically lax by most archconservatives). The second edition was edited by Sir Ernest Gowers, who, to Fowler's original entry for *and* in the first edition, added this:

   That it is a solecism to begin a sentence with *and* is a faintly lingering superstition. (p. 29)

   To the original entry for *but,* he added "see *and.*" Some inexperienced writers do begin too many sentences with *and,* but that is an error not in grammar but of style.

Some insecure writers also think they should not begin a sentence with *because*. Not this:

✓ **Because** we have access to so much historical fact, today we know a good deal about changes within the humanities which were not apparent to those of any age much before our own and which the individual scholar must constantly reflect on.

—Walter Ong, S. J., "The Expanding Humanities and the Individual Scholar," *Publication of the Modern Language Association*

This folklore about *because* appears in no handbook, but it is gaining popular currency. It probably stems from advice aimed at avoiding sentence fragments like this one:

The plan was rejected. **Because** it was incomplete.

While this rule has no basis in grammar, it does reflect a small truth about style. In Lesson 5, we look at a principle of style that tells us to arrange the elements of a sentence so that information readers already know comes *before* information they don't. It is a fact of English style that a subordinate clause beginning with *because* usually introduces new information:

✓ Some writers write graceless prose **because** they are seized by the idea that writing is good only when it's free of errors that only a grammarian can explain.

Reverse that order and you get a mildly awkward sentence:

Because some writers are seized by the idea that writing is good only when it's free of errors that only a grammarian can explain, they write graceless prose.

When a *because*-clause introduces new information, don't put it at the beginning of a sentence; put it at the end. That, however, is not a rule of grammar, but rather a principle of style.

When you *begin* a sentence with a clause expressing causation and your reader is familiar with its substance, introduce the clause not with *because* but with *since,* because *since* implies that the reader already knows what is in the clause:

✓ Since our language seems to reflect our quality of mind, it is easy for those inclined to look down on others to think that grammatical "errors" indicate mental or moral deficiency.

When you put a *since*-clause at the *end* of a sentence, the sentence ends weakly.

It is easy for those inclined to look down on others to think that grammatical "errors" indicate mental or moral deficiency, **since** our language seems to reflect our quality of mind.

As with all principles, there are exceptions to this one, but it's generally sound.

2. **"Use the relative pronoun *that*—not *which*—for restrictive clauses."** Allegedly, not this:

✓ Next is a typical situation **which** a practiced writer corrects "for style" virtually by reflex action.

—Jacques Barzun, *Simple and Direct* (p. 69)

Yet just a few sentences before, Barzun himself, an eminent critic of style and historian of intellectual history asserted,

Us[e] *that* with defining [i.e., restrictive] clauses except when stylistic reasons interpose.

(In his sentence quoted above, no such reasons interpose.)

A rule has no force when someone like Barzun asserts it on one page, violates it on the next, and his "error" is never caught, not by his editors, not by his proofreaders, not even by Barzun himself.

This "rule" is relatively new. It appeared in 1906 in Henry and Francis Fowler's *The King's English* (Oxford University Press; reprinted as an Oxford University Press paperback, 1973). The Fowlers thought that the random variation between *that* and *which* was messy, so they just asserted that writers should (with some exceptions) limit *which* to *nonrestrictive* clauses.

A nonrestrictive clause, you may recall, modifies a noun naming a referent that you can identify unambiguously without the added information in that clause. For example,

✓ ABC Inc. ended its first bankruptcy, **which** it filed in 2006.

A company can have only one first bankruptcy, so we can unambiguously identify the bankruptcy mentioned without the information in the following clause. We therefore call that clause *nonrestrictive*, because it does not "restrict" or uniquely identify what the noun phrase names, *its first bankruptcy*. In that context, we put a comma before the modifying clause and begin it with *which*. That rule is based on both historical and contemporary usage.

But, claimed the Fowlers, for restrictive clauses, we should use not *which* but only *that*: For example,

✓ ABCO Inc. sold a product **that** [*not **which***] made millions.

Since ABCO presumably makes many products, the clause *that made millions* "restricts" the product to only the one that made millions, and so, said the Fowlers, it should begin with *that*.

Francis died in 1918, but Henry continued the family tradition with *A Dictionary of Modern English Usage*. In that landmark work, he discussed the finer points of *which* and *that*, then added this:

> Some there are who follow this principle now; but it would be idle to pretend that it is the practice either of most or of the best writers. (p. 635)

That wistful comment was kept in the second edition and again in the third. (For another allegedly incorrect *which*, see the passage by Walter Ong on p. 13.)

I confess I follow Fowler's advice, not because a restrictive *which* is wrong, but because *that* is softer. I do sometimes choose a *which* when it's within a word or two of a *that*, because I don't like the sound of two *that*s close together:

✓ I have **that** one rule **that** I will not give up.

✓ I have **that** one rule **which** I will not give up.

3. **"Use *fewer* with nouns you count, *less* with nouns you cannot."** Allegedly not this:

> ✓ I can remember no **less** than five occasions when the correspondence columns of *The Times* rocked with volleys of letters. . . .
>
> —Noel Gilroy Annan, Lord Annan, "The Life of the Mind in British Universities Today," *American Council of Learned Societies Newsletter*

No one uses *fewer* with mass nouns (*fewer dirt*), but educated writers often use *less* with countable plural nouns (*less resources*).

4. **"Use *since* and *while* to refer only to time, not to mean *because* or *although*."** Most careful writers use *since* with a meaning close to *because* but, as mentioned above, with an added sense of 'What follows I assume you already know':

✓ **Since** asbestos causes cancer, handle it carefully.

Nor do most careful writers restrict *while* to its temporal sense (*We'll wait while you eat*). They also use it with a meaning close to 'I assume you know what I state in this clause, but I will qualify it with what I assert in the next:

✓ **While** we agree on a date, we disagree about the place.

In both cases, put the clause first in a sentence, because both *since* and *while* imply that the reader already knows what is in a clause they introduce. When you put such a clause last, the sentence ends lamely:

> Asbestos should be removed carefully, since it is dangerous.
>
> We disagree about the place, while we agree on a date.

> *Here's the point:*   When competent writers regularly violate an alleged rule and most careful readers never notice, then the rule has no force. In those cases, it is not writers who should obey the grammarians, but the grammarians who should change their rules.

Elegant Options

These next "rules" complement the Real Rules: call them *Elegant Options*. Most readers do not notice when you observe a Real Rule, but does when you violates it (like that). On the other hand, few readers notice when you violate one of these optional rules, but some do when you observe it, because doing so makes your writing seem slightly more formal.

1. **"Don't split infinitives."** Purists condemn Dwight MacDonald, a linguistic archconservative, for this sentence:

   ✓ One wonders why Dr. Gove and his editors did not think of labeling *knowed* as substandard right where it occurs, and one suspects that they wanted **to slightly conceal** the fact. . . .

   —"The String Untuned," *The New Yorker*

   They would require

   they wanted **to conceal slightly** the fact . . .

   Infinitives are now split so often that when you self-consciously avoid splitting one, careful readers may think you are trying to be especially correct, whether you are or not.

2. **"Use *whom* as the object of a verb or preposition."** Purists would condemn William Zinsser for this *who:*

   ✓ Soon after you confront this matter of preserving your identity, another question will occur to you: "**Who** am I writing for?"

   —*On Writing Well*

They would insist on

> . . . another question will occur to you: "For **whom** am I writing?"

Most readers take *whom* as a sign of deliberate correctness, so when a writer uses it incorrectly, that choice is probably a sign of insecurity:

> The committee must decide **whom** should be promoted.

In that sentence, *whom* is the subject of the verb *should be promoted*, so it should be *who*. Here is an actual rule: Use *who* when it is the subject of a verb *in its own clause;* use *whom* only when it is an object in its own clause, as in

> The committee must decide **whom** it should hire.

3. **"Don't end a sentence with a preposition."** Purists condemn Sir Ernest Gowers, editor of Fowler's second edition, for this:

> ✓ The peculiarities of legal English are often used as a stick to beat the official **with.**

> —*The Complete Plain Words*

and insist on this:

> . . . a stick **with which** to beat the official.

The first is correct; the second more formal. (Again, see the Ong passage on p. 13.) And your sentence will seem more formal yet if you shift both the preposition and its *whom* to the left. Compare:

> ✓ The man I met **with** was the man I had written **to.**

> ✓ The man **with whom** I met was the man **to whom** I had written.

A final preposition can, however, end a sentence weakly (see pp. 120–121). George Orwell may have chosen to end this next sentence with *from* to make a sly point about English grammar, but I suspect it just ended up there (and note the "incorrect" *which*):

> [The defense of the English language] has nothing to do with . . . the setting up of a "standard English" **which** must never be departed **from.**

> —George Orwell, "Politics and the English Language"

This would have been less awkward and more emphatic:

> We do not defend English just to create a "standard English" whose rules we must always obey.

4. **"Use the singular with *none* and *any*."** *None* and *any* were originally singular, but today most writers use them as plural, so if you use them as singular, some readers will notice. The second sentence below is a bit more formal than the first:

✓ **None** of the reasons **are** sufficient to end the project.

✓ **None** of the reasons **is** sufficient to end the project.

When you are under close scrutiny by very careful readers, you might choose to observe all these optional rules. Ordinarily, though, they are ignored by most careful writers, which is to say they are not rules at all, but rather stylistic choices that create a slightly formal tone. If you adopt the worst-case approach and observe them all, all the time—well, private virtues are their own reward.

Hobgoblins

For some reason, a handful of items has become the object of particularly zealous abuse. There's no explaining why; none of them interferes with clarity or concision.

1. **"Never use *like* for *as* or *as if*."** Not this:

✓ These operations failed **like** the earlier ones did.

But this:

✓ These operations failed **as** the earlier ones did.

Like became a subordinating conjunction in the eighteenth century when writers began to drop *as* from the phrase *like as,* leaving just *like* as the conjunction. This process is called *elision,* a common linguistic change. It is telling that the editor of the second edition of Fowler (the one favored by conservatives) deleted *like* for *as* from Fowler's list of "Illiteracies" and moved it into the category of "Sturdy Indefensibles."

2. **"Don't use *hopefully* to mean 'I hope.'"** Not this:

   ✓ Hopefully, it will not rain.

   But this:

   ✓ It is hoped that it will not rain.

   This "rule" dates from about the middle of the twentieth century; it has no basis in logic or grammar. It parallels the use of other words that no one abuses, words such as *candidly, frankly, sadly,* and *happily:*

   ✓ Candidly, we may fail. (That is, *I am candid when I say . . .*)

   ✓ Seriously, we must go. (That is, *I am serious when I say . . .*)

3. **"Don't use *finalize* to mean 'finish' or 'complete.'"** But *finalize* doesn't mean just 'finish.' It means 'to clean up the last few details,' a sense captured by no other word. Moreover, if we think *finalize* is bad because *-ize* is ugly, we would have to reject *nationalize, synthesize,* and *rationalize,* along with hundreds of other words.

4. **"Don't use *impact* as a verb, as in *The survey* impacted *our strategy.* Use it only as a noun, as in *The survey had* an impact *on our strategy.*"** *Impact* has been a verb for 400 years, but on some people, historical evidence has none.

5. **"Don't modify absolute words such as *perfect, unique, final,* or *complete* with *very, more, quite,* and so on."** That rule would have ruled out this familiar sentence:

   ✓ We the People of the United States, in order to form a **more perfect** union. . . . (Even so, this is a rule worth following.)

6. **"Never ever use *irregardless* for *regardless* or *irrespective*."** However arbitrary this rule is, follow it. Use *irregardless* and by some you will be judged irredeemable.

Words That Attract Special Attention

Some words are so often confused with others that careful readers are likely to note your care when you correctly distinguish them—*flaunt* and *flout*, for example. Those who think the difference matters are likely to think that at least *you* know that *flaunt* means 'to display conspicuously' and that *flout* means 'to scorn a rule or standard.' Thus if you chose to scorn the distinction, you would not flout your flaunting it, but flaunt your flouting it. Here are some others:

aggravate means 'to make worse.' It does not mean to 'annoy.' You can aggravate an injury but not a person.

anticipate means 'to prepare for a contingency.' It does not mean just 'expect.' You anticipate a question when you prepare its answer before it's asked; if you know it's coming but don't prepare, you only expect it.

anxious means 'uneasy' not 'eager.' You're eager to leave if you're happy to. You're anxious about leaving if it makes you nervous.

blackmail means 'to extort by threatening to reveal damaging information.' It does not mean simply 'coerce.' One country cannot blackmail another with nuclear weapons when it only threatens to use them.

cohort means 'a group who attends on someone.' It does not mean a single accompanying person. When Prince Charles married his friend she became his 'consort'; his hangers-on are still his cohort.

comprise means 'to include all parts in one unit.' It is not synonymous with *constitute*. The alphabet is not comprised *by* its letters; it comprises them. Letters *constitute* the alphabet, which is thus constituted by them.

continuous means 'without interruption.' It is not synonymous with *continual*, which means an activity through time, with interruptions. If you *continuously* interrupt someone, that person will never say a word because your interruption will never stop. If you *continually* interrupt, you let the other person finish a sentence from time to time.

disinterested means 'neutral.' It does not mean 'uninterested.' A judge should be disinterested in the outcome of a case, but not uninterested in it. (Incidentally, the original meaning of *disinterested* was 'to be uninterested.')

enormity means 'hugely bad.' It does not mean 'enormous.' In private, a belch might be enormous, but at a state funeral, it would also be an enormity.

fortuitous means 'by chance.' It does not mean 'fortunate.' You are fortunate when you fortuitously pick the right number in a lottery.

fulsome means 'sickeningly excessive.' It does not mean just 'much.' We all enjoy praise, except when it becomes fulsome.

notorious means 'known for bad behavior.' It does not mean 'famous.' Frank Sinatra was a famous singer but a notorious bully.

To be sure, these days only a few readers care about these distinctions, but they may be just those whose judgment carries special weight when it matters the most. So it may be worth learning to distinguish these words, especially if you also think their differences are worth preserving.

On the other hand, you get no points for correctly distinguishing *imply* and *infer*, *principal* and *principle*, *accept* and *except*, *capital* and *capitol*, *affect* and *effect*, *proceed* and *precede*, *discrete* and *discreet*. That's just expected of a careful writer. Most careful readers also notice when a Latinate or Greek plural noun is used as a singular, so you might want to keep these straight, too:

Singular	datum	criterion	medium	stratum	phenomenon
Plural	data	criteria	media	strata	phenomena

> *Here's the point:*   You can't predict correct usage by logic or general rule. You have to learn the rules one-by-one and accept the fact that most of them are arbitrary and idiosyncratic.

A Problem: Pronouns and Gender Bias

We expect literate writers to make verbs agree with subjects:

✓ Our **reasons** ARE based on solid evidence.

We also expect pronouns to agree with antecedents. Not this:

> Early **efforts** to oppose the hydrogen bomb failed because **it** ignored political issues. **No one** wanted to expose **themselves** to anti-Communist hysteria.

But this:

✓ Early **efforts** to oppose the hydrogen bomb failed because **they** ignored political issues. **No one** wanted to expose **himself** to anti-Communist hysteria.

There are, however, two problems.

First, do we use a singular or plural pronoun when we refer to singular nouns that are plural in meaning, such as a *group, committee, staff, administration,* and so on. And do we use a singular or plural verb? Some writers use a singular verb and pronoun when the group acts as a single entity:

✓ The **committee** HAS met but has not yet made **its** decision.

But they use a plural verb and pronoun when its members act individually:

✓ The **faculty** HAVE the memo, but not all of **them** have read it.

These days plurals are irregularly used in both senses (the plural is the rule in British English).

Second, what pronoun do we use, *it* or *they*, to refer to pronouns such as *someone, everyone, no one* and to singular nouns that do not indicate gender: *teacher, doctor, student*? We casually use *they:*

> **Everyone** knows **they** must answer for **their** actions.
>
> When **a person** is on drugs, it is hard to help **them.**

Formal usage requires a singular pronoun:

> **Everyone** realizes that **he** must answer for **his actions.**

But that rule raises the problem of biased language.

Common sense demands that we not gratuitously offend readers, but if we reject *he* as a generic pronoun because it's biased and *they* because some readers consider it ungrammatical, we are left with several bad choices. Some writers choose a clumsy *he or she;* others choose a worse *he/she* or even *s/he.*

> If **a writer** ignores the ethnicity of **his or her** readers, **s/he** may respond in ways **the writer** would not expect to words that to **him or her** are unbiased.

Some writers substitute plurals for singulars:

> ✓ When **writers** ignore **their** readers' ethnicity, **they** may respond in ways **they** might not expect to words that are to **them** unbiased.

But in that sentence, *they, their,* and *them* are confusing, because they refer to two different referents. And to the careful ear, a sentence with singular nouns and pronouns seems a shade more precise than one with plurals. Compare the sentence above with this one:

> When a **writer** ignores **his** reader's ethnicity, **his reader** may respond in ways that **the writer** might not expect to words that are to **him** unbiased.

We can try a first person *we:*

> ✓ If **we** ignore the ethnicity of **our** readers, they may respond in ways **we** would not expect to words that to **us** are unbiased.

But *we* can also be ambiguous. We could also try impersonal abstraction, but that creates its own problem:

> Failure to consider ethnicity may lead to unexpected responses to words considered unbiased.

Finally, we can alternately use *he* and *she*, as I have. But that's not a perfect solution either, because some readers find *she* as stylistically intrusive as *he/she*. A reviewer in the *New York Times*, for example, wondered what to make of an author whom the reviewer charged with attempting to

> right history's wrongs to women by referring to random examples as "she," as in "Ask a particle physicist what happens when a quark is knocked out of a proton, and she will tell you ...," which strikes this reader as oddly patronizing to women.

(We might wonder how it strikes a woman who happens to be a particle physicist.)

Some writers use *one:*

> If **one** ignores the ethnicity of **one's** readers, they may respond in ways **one** would not expect to words that **one** thinks are unbiased.

But that's stilted.

For years to come, we'll have a problem with **singular** generic pronouns, and to some readers, any solution will be awkward. I suspect that eventually we will accept the plural *they* as a correct singular.

✓ **No one** should turn in **their** writing unedited.

Some claim that such compromises lead to lazy imprecision. Whatever the future, we have a choice now, and that's not a bad thing, because our choices define who we are, even when they are not based on logical principles. As E. B. White once said about "good grammar,"

> English usage is sometimes more than mere taste, judgment, and education—sometimes it's sheer luck, like getting across the street.

3

Actions

*Everything that can be thought at all
can be thought clearly.
Everything that can be said can be said clearly.*
—LUDWIG WITTGENSTEIN

MAKING JUDGMENTS

We have words enough to praise writing we like: *clear, direct, concise,* and more than enough to abuse writing we don't: *unclear, indirect, abstract, dense, complex.* We can use those words to distinguish these two sentences:

    1a. The cause of our schools' failure at teaching basic skills is not understanding the influence of cultural background on learning.

    1b. Our schools have failed to teach basic skills because they do not understand how cultural background influences the way a child learns.

Most of us would call (1a) dense and complex, (1b) clearer, more direct. But those words don't refer to anything *in* those sentences; they refer to how those sentences make us *feel*. When we say that (1a) is *unclear,* we mean that *we* had a hard time understanding it; we say it's *dense* when *we* have to struggle through it.

The problem is to understand what is *in* those two sentences that makes us feel as we do. Only then can you avoid your too-good understanding of your own writing to know when readers will think it needs revising. To do that, you have to know what counts as a well-told story.

LINKING CHARACTERS TO THEIR ACTIONS

It is easy to state the most general principle of clarity: Make the main character in your sentence its subject and make its important actions verbs. This story doesn't do that:

> 2a. Once upon a time, as a walk through the woods was taking place on the part of Little Red Riding Hood, the Wolf's jump out from behind a tree occurred, causing her fright.

We prefer a sentence closer to this (the check indicates not correctness but the clearer sentence):

> ✓ 2b. Once upon a time, Little Red Riding Hood was walking through the woods, when the Wolf jumped out from behind a tree and frightened her.

Most readers think (2b) is clearer than (2a), because it follows two principles that (2a) ignores:

- Its main characters are subjects of verbs.
- Those verbs express specific actions.

Two definitions: To understand those two principles, we have to distinguish simple subjects from whole subjects. The simple subject of a sentence is the noun or nouns that determine whether a verb is singular or plural:

>   singular subject   singular verb
> The   <u>evidence</u>   that you offer   <u>is</u>   not reliable.

The *whole* subject is the simple subject and everything attached to it:

>   whole subject
> <u>The evidence that you offer</u> is not reliable.

Principle of Clarity 1: Make Main Characters Subjects

Look at the subjects in (2a). The simple subjects (boldfaced) are *not* the main characters (italicized):

2a. Once upon a time, as a **walk** through the woods was taking place on the part of *Little Red Riding Hood, the Wolf's* **jump** out from behind a tree occurred, causing *her* fright.

Those subjects do not name characters; they name actions expressed in abstract nouns, *walk* and *jump:*

SUBJECT	VERB
a **walk** through the woods	was taking place
the *Wolf's* **jump** out from behind a tree	occurred

The *whole* subject of *occurred* does have a character *in* it: *the **Wolf's** jump,* but *the Wolf* is only attached to the simple subject *jump;* it is not *the* simple subject.

Contrast those abstract subjects with the concrete subjects (italicized and boldfaced) in (2b):

✓ 2b. Once upon a time, ***Little Red Riding Hood*** was walking through the woods, when ***the Wolf*** jumped out from behind a tree and frightened *her.*

The subjects and the main characters are now the same words:

SUBJECT/CHARACTER	VERB
Little Red Riding Hood	was walking
the Wolf	jumped

Principle of Clarity 2: Make Important Actions Verbs

Now look at how the actions and verbs differ in (2a): its actions are not in verbs but in abstract nouns (actions are boldfaced; verbs are capitalized):

2a. Once upon a time, as a **walk** through the woods WAS TAKING place on the part of Little Red Riding Hood, the Wolf's **jump** out from behind a tree OCCURRED, causing **her fright.**

Note how vague those verbs are: *was taking, occurred.* In (2b), the clearer sentence, the verbs name specific actions:

✓ 2b. Once upon a time, Little Red Riding Hood WAS **WALKING** through the woods, when the Wolf **JUMPED** out from behind a tree and **FRIGHTENED** her.

Here's the point: In (2a), the sentence that seems wordy and indirect, the two main characters are Little Red Riding Hood and the Wolf, but they are *not* subjects, and their actions—*walk, jump,* and *fright*—are *not* verbs. In (2b), the more direct sentence, those two main characters *are* subjects and those three actions *are* verbs. That's why we prefer (2b).

FAIRY TALES AND ACADEMIC WRITING

Fairy tales seem distant from writing in college or on the job, but they're not, because most sentences are still about characters doing things. Compare these two:

3a. The Federalists' argument in regard to the destabilization of government by popular democracy was based on their belief in the tendency of factions to further their self-interest at the expense of the common good.

✓ 3b. The Federalists argued that popular democracy destabilized government, because they believed that factions tended to further their self-interest at the expense of the common good.

We can analyze those sentences as we did the ones about Little Red Riding Hood.

Sentence (3a) feels dense for two reasons. First, its characters are not subjects. The simple subject is *argument,* but the characters are *Federalists, popular democracy, government,* and *factions* (characters are italicized; the simple subject is boldfaced):

> 3a. *The Federalists'* **argument** in regard to the destabilization of *government* by *popular democracy* was based on *their* belief in the tendency of *factions* to further *their* self-interest at the expense of the common good.

Second, most of the actions (boldfaced) are not verbs (capitalized), but rather abstract nouns (boldfaced). And neither of the verbs (capitalized) are actions.

> 3a. The Federalists' **argument** in regard to the **destabilization** of government by popular democracy WAS BASED on their **belief** in the **tendency** of factions to FURTHER their self-interest at the expense of the common good.

Especially notice the long subject of (3a) and how little meaning is expressed by its main verb *was based:*

WHOLE SUBJECT	VERB
The Federalists' argument in regard to the destabilization of government by popular democracy	was based

Readers think (3b) is clearer for two reasons: first, its characters (italicized) *are* subjects (boldfaced):

> 3b. The ***Federalists*** argued that ***popular democracy*** destabilized government, because ***they*** believed that ***factions*** tended to further *their* self-interest at the expense of the common good.

Second, the actions (boldfaced) are verbs (capitalized):

> 3b. The Federalists ARGUED that popular democracy DESTABILIZED government, because they BELIEVED that factions TENDED to FURTHER their self-interest at the expense of the common good.

Note as well that all those whole subjects are short, specific, and concrete:

WHOLE SUBJECT/CHARACTER	VERB/ACTION
the Federalists	argued
popular democracy	destabilized
they	believed
factions	tended to further

In the rest of this lesson, we look at actions and verbs; in the next, at characters and subjects.

VERBS AND ACTIONS

Our principle is this: *A sentence seems clear when its important actions are in verbs.* Look at how sentences (4a) and (4b) express their actions. In (4a), the actions (boldfaced) are not verbs (capitalized); they are nouns:

> 4a. Our **lack** of data PREVENTED **evaluation** of our **actions** in **targeting** funds to areas in **need** of **assistance.**

In (4b), on the other hand, the actions are almost all verbs:

> ✓4b. Because we **LACKED** data, we could not **EVALUATE** whether we **HAD TARGETED** funds to areas that **NEEDED** **assistance.**

Readers will think your writing is dense if you use lots of abstract nouns, especially those derived from verbs and adjectives, nouns ending in *-tion, -ment, -ence,* and so on, *especially when you make those abstract nouns the subjects of verbs.*

A noun derived from a verb or adjective has a technical name: *nominalization.* The word illustrates its meaning: when we nominalize the verb *nominalize,* we create the nominalization *nominalization.* A few examples:

VERB → NOMINALIZATION		ADJECTIVE → NOMINALIZATION	
discover	→ discovery	careless	→ carelessness
resist	→ resistance	different	→ difference
react	→ reaction	proficient	→ proficiency

We can also nominalize a verb by adding *-ing* (making it a gerund):

She flies → her flying   We sang → our singing

Some nominalizations and verbs are identical:

hope → hope   result → result   repair → repair

We **REQUEST** that you **REVIEW** the data.

Our **request** IS that you DO a **review** of the data.

(Some actions also hide out in adjectives: *It is applicable →
it applies*. Some others: *indicative, dubious, argumentative,
deserving.*)

No element of style more characterizes turgid academic and
bureaucratic writing, writing that feels abstract, indirect, and difficult, than lots of nominalizations, *especially in the subjects of verbs*.

Here's the point: In grade school, we learned that
subjects *are* characters (or "doers") and that verbs *are* actions. That's often true:

subject	verb	object
We	discussed	the problem.
doer	action	

But it is not true for this almost synonymous sentence:

subject	verb		
The problem	was	the topic	of our discussion.
		doer	action

We can move characters and actions around in a sentence, and subjects and verbs don't have to be any particular thing at all. But when in most of your sentences you
put characters in subjects and actions in verbs, readers
are likely to think your prose is clear, direct, and readable.

DIAGNOSIS AND REVISION

You can use the principles of verbs as actions and subjects as characters to explain why your readers judge your prose as they do. But more important, you can also use them to identify and revise sentences that your readers will think are wordy and dense. Revision is a three-step process: diagnose, analyze, rewrite.

1. **Diagnose**
   a. Ignoring short (four- or five-word) introductory phrases, underline the first seven or eight words in each sentence.

      <u>The outsourcing of high-tech work to Asia by</u> corporations means the loss of jobs for many American workers.

   b. Then look for two things:
      - You underlined abstract nouns as simple subjects (boldfaced).

        The **outsourcing** of high-tech work to Asia by corporations means the loss of jobs for many American workers.

      - You read seven or eight words before getting to a verb.

        <u>The outsourcing of high-tech work to Asia by corporations</u> (10 words) means the loss of jobs for many American workers.

2. **Analyze**
   a. Decide who your main characters are, particularly flesh-and-blood (more about this in the next lesson).

      The outsourcing of high-tech work to Asia by **corporations** means the loss of jobs for **many American workers.**

   b. Then look for the actions that those characters perform, especially actions in those abstract nouns derived from verbs.

      The **outsourcing** of high-tech work to Asia by corporations means the **loss** of jobs for many American workers.

3. **Rewrite**

   a. If the actions are nominalizations, make them verbs.

   outsourcing → outsource   loss → lose

   b. Make the characters the subjects of those verbs.

   corporations outsource   American workers lose

   c. Rewrite the sentence with subordinating conjunctions such as *because, if, when, although, why, how, whether,* or *that.*

   Many middle-class American workers are losing their jobs, **because** corporations are outsourcing their high-tech work to Asia.

SOME COMMON PATTERNS

You can quickly spot and revise five common patterns of nominalizations.

1. **The nominalization is the subject of an empty verb such as *be, seems, has,* etc.:**

   The **intention** of the committee is to audit the records.

   a. Change the nominalization to a verb:

   intention → intend

   b. Find a character that would be the subject of that verb:

   The intention of **the committee** is to audit the records.

   c. Make that character the subject of the verb:

   The committee INTENDS to audit the records.

2. **The nominalization follows an empty verb:**

   The *agency* CONDUCTED an **investigation** into the matter.

a. Change the nominalization to a verb:

> investigation → investigate

b. Replace the empty verb with the new verb:

> conducted → investigated

> ✓ The *agency* **INVESTIGATED** the matter.

3. **One nominalization is a subject of an empty verb and a second nominalization follows it:**

Our **loss** in sales WAS a result of their **expansion** of outlets.

a. Revise the nominalizations into verbs:

> loss → lose   expansion → expand

b. Identify the characters that would be the subjects of those verbs:

Our loss in sales was a result of **their** expansion of outlets.

c. Make those characters subjects of those verbs:

> we lose   they expand

d. Link the new clauses with a logical connection:

- To express simple cause: *because, since, when*
- To express conditional cause: *if, provided that, so long as*
- To contradict expected causes: *though, although, unless*

> Our **loss** in sales   → *We* **LOST** sales
> was the result of   → **BECAUSE**
> their **expansion** of outlets → *they* **EXPANDED** outlets

4. **A nominalization follows *there is* or *there are*:**

There IS no **need** for *our* further **study** of this problem.

    a. Change the nominalization to a verb:

        need → need   study → study

    b. Identify the character that should be the subject of the verb:

        There is no need for **our** further study of this problem.

    c. Make that character the subject of the verb:

         no need → we need not   our study → we study

        We **NEED** not **STUDY** this problem further.

5. **Two or three nominalizations in a row are joined by prepositions:**

    We did a **review** of the **evolution** of the brain.

    a. Turn the first nominalization into a verb:

        review → review

    b. Either leave the second nominalization as it is or turn it into a verb in a clause beginning with *how* or *why*:

        evolution of the brain → how the brain evolved

        First, *we* **REVIEWED** the **evolution** of the *brain*.

    ✓ First, *we* **REVIEWED** how *the brain* **EVOLVED.**

SOME HAPPY CONSEQUENCES

When you consistently rely on verbs to express key actions, your readers benefit in many ways:

1. Your sentences are more concrete. Compare:

    There WAS an affirmative **decision** for **expansion.**
    ✓ *The director* **DECIDED** to **EXPAND** the program.

2. Your sentences are more concise. When you use nominalizations, you have to add articles like *a* and *the* and prepositions

such as *of, by,* and *in.* You don't need them when you use verbs:

> A **revision** *of* the program WILL RESULT *in* **increases** *in* our **efficiency** *in the* **servicing** *of* clients.
>
> ✓ If we REVISE the program, we CAN SERVE clients more EFFICIENTLY.

3. The logic of your sentences is clearer. When you nominalize verbs, you have to link actions with fuzzy prepositions and phrases such as *of, by,* and *on the part of.* But when you use verbs, you link clauses with precise subordinating conjunctions such as *because, although,* and *if:*

> Our more effective presentation of our study resulted in our success, despite an earlier start by others.
>
> ✓ **Although** others started earlier, we succeeded **because** we presented our study more effectively.

4. Your sentence tells a more coherent story. This next sequence of actions distorts their chronology. (The numbers refer to the real sequence of events.)

> Decisions[4] in regard to administration[5] of medication despite inability[2] of an irrational patient appearing[1] in a Trauma Center to provide legal consent[3] rest with the attending physician alone.

When we revise those actions into verbs and reorder them, we get a more coherent narrative:

> ✓ When a patient appears[1] in a Trauma Center and behaves[2] so irrationally that he cannot legally consent[3] to treatment, only the attending physician can decide[4] whether to medicate[5] him.

A QUALIFICATION: USEFUL NOMINALIZATIONS

I have so relentlessly urged you to turn nominalizations into verbs that you might think you should never use them. But in fact, you can't write well without them. The trick is to know which nominalizations to keep and which to revise. Keep these:

1. **A nominalization as a short subject refers to a previous sentence:**

   ✓ **These arguments** all depend on a single unproven claim.

   ✓ **This decision** can lead to positive outcomes.

   Those nominalizations link one sentence to another in a cohesive flow, an issue I'll discuss in more detail in Lesson 5.

2. **A short nominalization replaces an awkward *The fact that*:**

   The fact that she ADMITTED her guilt impressed me.

   ✓ Her **acknowledgment** of her guilt impressed me.

   But then, why not this:

   ✓ *She* IMPRESSED me when *she* ADMITTED her guilt.

3. **A nominalization names what would be the object of the verb:**

   I accepted *what she* REQUESTED [that is, *She requested **something***].

   ✓ I accepted her **request.**

   However, contrast *request* above with this next sentence, where *request* is more of an action:

   Her **request** for **assistance** CAME after the deadline.

   ✓ She REQUESTED assistance after the deadline.

4. **A nominalization refers to a concept so familiar to your readers that to them, it is a character (more on this in Lesson 4):**

   ✓ Few problems have so divided us as **abortion** on **demand.**

   ✓ The Equal Rights **Amendment** was an issue in past **elections.**

   ✓ **Taxation** without **representation** did not spark the American **Revolution.**

Those nominalizations name familiar concepts: *abortion* on *demand, amendment, election, taxation, representation, revolution.* You must develop an eye for nominalizations expressing a familiar idea and those that you can revise into a verb:

There is a **demand** for a **repeal** of the car tax.

✓ We DEMAND that the government REPEAL the car tax.

Shakespeare's Hamlet had acting style in mind when he told the actors in the play-within-the-play how they should act their parts, but his advice also applies to how we should write our sentences:

Suit the action to the word, the word to the action.

—Hamlet, 3.2

4

Characters

When character is lost, all is lost.
—Anonymous

UNDERSTANDING THE IMPORTANCE OF CHARACTERS

Readers think sentences are clear and direct when they see key actions in their verbs. Compare (1a) with (1b):

1a. The CIA feared the president would recommend to Congress that it reduce its budget.

1b. The CIA had fears that the president would send a recommendation to Congress that it make reductions in its budget.

Sentence (1a) is a third shorter than (1b), but some readers don't think it's a great deal clearer.

But now compare (1b) and (1c):

1b. The CIA had fears that the president would send a recommendation to Congress that it make reductions in its budget.

1c. The fear of the CIA was that a recommendation from the president to Congress would be for reductions in its budget.

Every reader thinks that (1c) is much less clear than either (1a) or (1b).

The reason is that in both (1a) and (1b), important characters are short, specific, concrete subjects of verbs (characters are italicized, simple subjects boldfaced, verbs capitalized):

1a. ***The CIA*** FEARED ***the president*** WOULD RECOMMEND to Congress that ***it*** REDUCE its budget.

1b. ***The CIA*** HAD fears that ***the president*** WOULD SEND a recommendation to Congress that ***it*** MAKE a reduction in its budget.

But the two subjects in (1c) are not concrete characters; they are abstractions (the simple subject is boldfaced; the whole subject is underlined).

1c. The **fear** of the *CIA* WAS that **a recommendation** from the *president to Congress* WOULD BE for **reductions** in its budget.

The different verbs in (1a) and (1b) make some difference, but the abstract subjects in (1c) make a bigger one.

Here's the point: Readers want actions in verbs, but *even more* they want characters as their subjects. We give readers a problem when for no good reason we do not name characters in subjects, or worse, delete them entirely, like this:

> There was fear that there would be a recommendation for a budget reduction.

Who fears? Who recommends? Who reduces? It is important to express actions in verbs, but the *first* principle of a clear style is this: Make the subjects of most of your verbs short, specific, and concrete.

DIAGNOSIS AND REVISION

Finding and Relocating Characters

To get characters into subjects, you have to know three things:

1. when you haven't done that
2. if you haven't, where you should look for characters
3. what you should do when you find them (or don't)

For example, this sentence feels indirect and impersonal.

> Governmental intervention in fast-changing technologies has led to the distortion of market evolution and interference in new product development.

We can diagnose that sentence:

1. **Skim the first seven or eight words:**

   > <u>Governmental intervention in fast-changing technologies has led</u> to the distortion of market evolution and interference in new product development.

   In those first words, readers want to see characters not just *in* the whole subjects of verbs, as **government** is implied in **governmental,** but *as* their simple subjects. In that example, however, they aren't.

2. **Find the main characters.** They may be possessive pronouns attached to nominalization, objects of prepositions (particularly *by* and *of*), or only implied. In that sentence, one main character is in the adjective *governmental;* the other, *market,* is in the object of a preposition: *of market evolution.*

3. **Skim the passage for actions involving those characters, particularly actions buried in nominalizations.** Ask *Who is doing what?*

governmental **intervention**	→	*government* **intervenes**
distortion	→	*[government]* **distorts**
market **evolution**	→	*markets* **evolve**
interference	→	*[government]* **interferes**
development	→	*[market]* **develops**

To revise, reassemble those new subjects and verbs into a sentence, using conjunctions such as *if, although, because, when, how,* and *why:*

✓ **When** a *government* **INTERVENES** in fast-changing technologies, *it* **DISTORTS** how *markets* **EVOLVE** or **INTERFERES** with their ability to **DEVELOP** new products.

Be aware that just as actions can be in adjectives (*reliable* →
rely), so can characters:

> Medieval *theological* debates often addressed issues considered
> trivial by modern *philosophical* thought.

When you find a character implied in an adjective, revise in the
same way:

> ✓ *Medieval theologians* often debated issues that *modern philoso-
> phers* consider trivial.

> ***Here's the point:***   The first step in diagnosing your
> style is to look at your subjects. If you do not see your
> main characters there in simple subjects, stated in a few
> short, concrete words, you have to look for them. They
> can be in objects of prepositions, in possessive pronouns,
> or in adjectives. Once you find them, look for actions they
> are involved in. Then make those characters the subjects
> of verbs naming those actions.

Reconstructing Absent Characters

Readers have the biggest problem with sentences devoid of
characters:

> A decision was made in favor of doing a study of the disagreements.

That sentence could mean either of these, and more:

> We decided that I should study why they disagreed.
>
> I decided that you should study why he disagreed.

The writer may know who is doing what, but readers might not
and so usually need help.

> Sometimes we omit characters to make a general statement.

> Research strategies that look for more than one variable are of more
> use in understanding factors in psychiatric disorder than strategies
> based on the assumption that the presence of psychopathology is

dependent on a single gene or on strategies in which only one bio-
logical variable is studied.

But when we try to revise that into something clearer, we have
to invent characters, then decide what to call them. Do we use
one or *we*, or name a generic "doer"?

> ✓ If *one/we/you/researchers* are to understand what causes psychiatric
> disorder, *one/we/you/they* should use research strategies that look
> for more than one variable rather than assume that a single gene is
> responsible for psychopathology or adopt a strategy in which
> *one/we/you//they* study only one biological variable.

To most of us, *one* feels stiff, but *we* may be ambiguous because
it can refer just to the writer, to the writer and others but not
the reader, to the reader and writer but not others, or to everyone. And if you are not directly naming your reader, *you* is usually inappropriate.

But if you avoid both nominalizations and vague pronouns,
you can slide into passive verbs (I'll discuss them in a moment):

> To understand what makes patients vulnerable to psychiatric
> disorders, strategies that look for more than one variable
> **SHOULD BE USED** rather than strategies in which it **IS ASSUMED**
> that a gene causes psychopathology or only one biological vari-
> able **IS STUDIED**.

This is a matter where judgment is important, but in general
look for the most specific character you can find.

In some cases, characters are so remote that you have to start
over:

> There are good reasons to account for the lack of evidence.

> ✓ I can explain why I have found no evidence.

Abstractions as Characters

So far, I've discussed characters as if they had to be flesh-and-
blood people. But you can tell stories whose main characters
are abstractions, including nominalizations, so long as you

make them the subjects of verbs that state specific actions involving those abstractions. Here's a story about a character called *freedom of speech*, two nominalizations.

> ✓ No right is more basic to a free society than **freedom of speech.**
> **Free speech** served the left in the 1960s when it protested the
> Vietnam War, and **it** is now used by the right when it claims that
> speech includes contributions to political organizations. **The doc-**
> **trine of free speech** has been embraced by all sides to protect
> themselves against those who would silence unpopular views. As a
> legal concept, **it** arose . . .

The phrase *freedom of speech* (or its equivalents *free speech* and *it*) is a virtual character because we are so familiar with it and because it is the subject of a series of actions such as *served, is used, has been embraced,* and *arose.*

But when you do use abstractions as characters, you can create a problem. A story about an abstraction as familiar as *free speech* is clear enough, but if you surround an unfamiliar abstract character with a lot of other abstractions, readers will feel that your writing is dense and complex.

For example, few of us are familiar with *prospective* and *immediate intention,* so most of us are likely to struggle with a story about them, especially when those terms are surrounded by other abstractions (actions are boldfaced; human characters are italicized):

> The **argument** is this. The cognitive component of **intention** ex-
> hibits a high degree of **complexity**. **Intention** is temporally divisi-
> ble into two: prospective **intention** and immediate **intention**. The
> cognitive function of prospective **intention** is the **representation**
> of a *subject*'s similar past **actions,** *his* current situation, and *his*
> course of future **actions.** That is, the cognitive component of
> prospective **intention** is a **plan.** The cognitive function of imme-
> diate **intention** is the **monitoring** and **guidance** of ongoing bod-
> ily **movement.**
>
> —Myles Brand, *Intending and Acting*

We can make that passage clearer if we tell it from the point of view of flesh-and-blood characters (they are italicized; "de-nominalized" verbs are boldfaced and capitalized):

✓ *I* **ARGUE** this about intention. It has a complex cognitive component of two temporal kinds: prospective and immediate. *We* use prospective intention to **REPRESENT** how *we* have **ACTED** in our past and present and how *we* will **ACT** in the future. That is, *we* use the cognitive component of prospective intention to help *us* **PLAN**. *We* use immediate intention to **MONITOR** and **GUIDE** *our* bodies as *we* **MOVE** them.

But have I made this passage say something that the writer didn't mean? Some argue that any change in form changes meaning. In this case, the writer might offer an opinion, but only his readers could decide whether the two passages have different meanings, because at the end of the day, a passage means not what the writer intended it to mean, but only what careful and competent readers think it does.

Here's the point: Most readers want the subjects of verbs to name the main characters in a story and those main characters to be flesh-and-blood. But often, you must write about abstractions. When you do, turn them into virtual characters by making them the subjects of verbs that tell a story. If readers are familiar with your abstractions, no problem. But when they are not, avoid using lots of other abstract nominalizations around them. When you revise an abstract passage, you may have a problem if the hidden characters are "people in general." You can try *we* or a general term for whoever is doing the action, such as *researchers, social critics, one,* and so on. But the fact is, unlike many other languages, English has no good stylistic solution for naming a generic "doer."

CHARACTERS AND PASSIVE VERBS

More than any other advice, you probably remember *Write in the active voice, not in the passive.* That's not bad advice, but it has exceptions.

When you write in the active voice, you typically put

- the agent or source of an action in the subject
- the goal or receiver of an action in a direct object:

	subject	verb	object
Active:	I	lost	the money.
	character/agent	action	goal

The passive differs in three ways:

1. The subject names the goal of the action.
2. A form of *be* precedes a verb in its past participle form.
3. The agent or source of the action is in a *by*-phrase or dropped entirely:

	subject	be + verb	prepositional phrase
Passive:	The money	was lost	[by me].
	goal	action	character/agent

The terms *active* and *passive*, however, are ambiguous, because they can refer not only to those two grammatical constructions but to how those sentences make you *feel*. We call a sentence *passive* if it feels flat, regardless of whether its verb is grammatically in the passive voice. For example, compare these two sentences.

We can manage problems if we control costs.

Problem management requires cost control.

Grammatically, both sentences are in the active voice, but the second *feels* passive, for three reasons:

- Neither of its actions—*management* and *control*—are verbs; both are nominalizations.

- The subject is *problem management,* an abstraction.
- The sentence lacks flesh-and-blood characters.

To understand why we respond to those two sentences as we do, we have to distinguish the literal meanings of *active* and *passive* from their figurative, impressionistic meanings.

Choosing Between Active and Passive

Some critics of style tell us to avoid the passive everywhere because it adds words and often deletes the agent, the "doer" of the action. But in fact, the passive is often the better choice. To choose between active and passive, you have to answer three questions:

1. **Must your readers know who is responsible for the action?** Often, we don't say who does an action, because we don't know or readers won't care. For example, we naturally choose the passive in these sentences:

   ✓ The president **WAS RUMORED** to have considered resigning.
   ✓ Those who **ARE FOUND** guilty can **BE FINED.**
   ✓ Valuable records should always **BE KEPT** in a safe.

   If we do not know who spread rumors, we cannot say, and no one doubts who finds people guilty or fines them or who should keep records safe. So those passives are the right choice.
      Sometimes, of course, writers use the passive when they don't want readers to know who did an action, especially when that doer is the writer. For example,

   Since the test was not done, the flaw was uncorrected.

   I will discuss the ethics of intended impersonality in Lesson 10.

2. **Would the active or passive verb help your readers move more smoothly from one sentence to the next?** We depend on the beginning of a sentence to give us a context of what we know before we follow the sentence to what's new.

A sentence confuses us when it opens with information that is unexpected. For example, in this next short passage, the subject of the second sentence gives us new and complex information (boldfaced), before we read more familiar information that we recall from the previous sentence (italicized):

> We must decide whether to improve education in the sciences alone or to raise the level of education across the whole curriculum. **The weight given to industrial competitiveness as opposed to the value we attach to the liberal arts**_{new information} will determine_{verb} *our decision*_{familiar information}.

In the second sentence, the verb *determine* is in the active voice: *will determine our decision*. But we could read the sentence more easily if it were passive, because the passive would put the short, familiar information (*our decision*) first and the newer, more complex information last, the order we all prefer:

> ✓ We must decide whether to improve education in the sciences alone or raise the level of education across the whole curriculum. *Our decision*_{familiar information} WILL BE DETERMINED_{passive verb} **by the weight we give to industrial competitiveness as opposed to the value we attach to the liberal arts**_{new information}.

(I discuss the issue of old and new more extensively in the next lesson.)

3. **Would the active or passive give readers a more consistent and appropriate point of view?** The writer of this next passage reports the end of World War II in Europe from the point of view of the Allies. To do so, she uses active verbs to make the Allies a consistent sequence of subjects:

> ✓ By early 1945, *the Allies* HAD essentially DEFEATED_{active} Germany; all that remained was a bloody climax. *American, French, British, and Russian forces* HAD BREACHED_{active} its borders and WERE BOMBING_{active} it around the clock. But *they* HAD not yet so DEVASTATED_{active} Germany as to destroy its ability to resist.

But had she wanted to explain history from the point of view of Germany, she would have used passive verbs to make Germany the subject/character:

✓ By early 1945, **Germany** HAD essentially BEEN DEFEATED_{passive;} all that remained was a bloody climax. **Its borders** HAD BEEN BREACHED_{passive,} and **it** WAS BEING BOMBED_{passive} around the clock. **It** HAD not BEEN SO DEVASTATED_{passive,} however, that **it** could not RESIST.

Some writers switch from one character to another for no apparent reason. Avoid this:

By early 1945, **the Allies** had essentially defeated Germany. **Its borders** had been breached, and **they** were bombing it around the clock. **Germany** was not so devastated, however, that **the Allies** would meet with no resistance. Though **Germany's population** was demoralized, **the Allies** still attacked their cities from the air.

Pick a point of view and stick to it.

Here's the point: Many writers use the passive verb too often, but it has its uses in these contexts:

- You don't know who did an action, readers don't care, or you don't want them to know.

- You want to shift a long bundle of information to the end of a sentence, especially when you can also move to its beginning a chunk of information that is shorter, more familiar, and therefore easier to grasp.

- You want your readers to focus on a particular character.

The "Objective" Passive vs. I/We

Some scholarly writers claim that they in particular should not use a first-person subject, because they must create an objective point of view, something like this:

Based on the writers' verbal intelligence, prior knowledge, and essay scores, their essays **were analyzed** for structure and evaluated for richness of concepts. The subjects **were** then **divided** into a high- or low-ability group. Half of each group **was** randomly **assigned** to a treatment group or to a placebo group.

Contrary to that claim, academic and scientific writers use the active voice and the first-person *I* and *we* regularly. These next passages come from articles in respected journals:

✓ This paper is concerned with two problems. How can **we** best handle in a transformational grammar certain restrictions that . . . , To illustrate, **we** may cite . . . , **we** shall show . . .

✓ Since the pituitary-adrenal axis is activated during the acute phase response, **we** have investigated the potential role . . . , Specifically, **we** have studied the effects of interleukin-1 . . .

Here are the first few words from several consecutive sentences from *Science,* a journal of great prestige:

✓ **We** examine . . . , **We** compare . . . , **We** have used . . . , Each has been weighted . . . , **We** merely take . . . , They are subject . . . , **We** use . . . , Elron and Morris describe . . . , **We** observed . . . , **We** might find . . .

—John P. Gilbert, Bucknam McPeek, and Frederick Mosteller, "Statistics and Ethics in Surgery and Anesthesia," *Science*

It is not true that academic writers always avoid the first-person *I* or *we*.

Passives, Characters, and Metadiscourse

When academic writers do use the first person, however, they use it in certain ways. There are two kinds:

• One kind refers directly to research activities: *study, investigate, examine, observe, use.* Those verbs are usually in the passive voice: *The subjects were observed* . . .

- The other kind of verb refers not to the activity of research, but to the writer's own writing and thinking: *cite, show, inquire.* These verbs are often active and in the first person: *We will show . . .* They are examples of what is called *metadiscourse.* Metadiscourse is language that refers not to the substance of your ideas, but to yourself, your reader, or your writing:

  - your thinking and act of writing: *We will explain, show, argue, claim, deny, suggest, contrast, add, expand, summarize . . .*
  - your readers' actions: *consider now, as you recall, look at the next example . . .*
  - the logic and form of what you have written: *first, second; to begin; therefore; however; consequently . . .*

Metadiscourse appears most often in introductions, where writers announce their intentions: *I claim that . . . , I will show . . . , We begin by . . . ,* and again at the end, when they summarize: *I have argued . . . , I have shown . . .* What distinguishes those actions is that only the writer can lay claim to them.

On the other hand, scholarly writers use the first person less often to describe specific actions they performed as *part* of their research, actions that anyone can perform. We rarely find passages like this:

> To determine if monokines elicited an adrenal steroidogenic response, **I** ADDED preparations of . . .

The writer of the original sentence used a passive verb, *were added,* to name an action that anyone can perform, not just the writer:

> To determine if monokines elicited a response, **preparations** . . . WERE ADDED.

But a problem lurks in a passive sentence like that: its writer dangled a modifier. You dangle a modifier when an introductory phrase has an *implied* subject that differs from the *explicit* subject in the following clause. In that example, the implied subject of the infinitive verb *determine* is *I* or *we: I determine* or *we determine.*

> [So that **I** could] determine if monokines elicited a response, preparations WERE ADDED.

But that *implied* subject, *I*, differs from the *explicit* subject of the clause it introduces—***preparations*** *were added.* When the implied and explicit subjects differ, the modifier dangles. Writers of scientific prose use this pattern so often, though, that it has become standard usage in their community.

We might note that this impersonal "scientific" style is a modern development. In his "New Theory of Light and Colors" (1672), Sir Isaac Newton wrote this charming first-person account of an experiment:

> I procured a triangular glass prism, to try therewith the celebrated phenomena of colors. And for that purpose, having darkened my laboratory, and made a small hole in my window shade, to let in a convenient quantity of the sun's light, I placed my prism at the entrance, that the light might be thereby refracted to the opposite wall. It was at first a very pleasing diversion to view the vivid and intense colors produced thereby.

Here's the point: Some writers and editors avoid the first person by using the passive everywhere, but deleting an *I* or *we* doesn't make a researcher's thinking more objective. We know that behind those impersonal sentences are flesh-and-blood people doing, thinking, and writing. In fact, the first-person *I* and *we* are common in scholarly prose when used with verbs that name actions unique to the writer.

NOUN + NOUN + NOUN

One more stylistic choice does not directly involve characters and actions, but we discuss it here because it can distort the match that readers expect between the form of an idea and the grammar of its expression. It is the long compound noun phrase:

> Early *childhood thought disorder misdiagnosis* often results from unfamiliarity with recent *research literature* describing such conditions. This paper reviews seven recent studies in which are findings of particular relevance to *pre-adolescent hyperactivity diagnosis* and to *treatment modalities* involving *medication maintenance level evaluation procedures.*

Some grammarians claim we should never modify one noun with another, but that would rule out common phrases such as *stone wall, student center, space shuttle,* and many other useful terms.

But strings of nouns feel lumpy, so avoid them, especially ones you invent. When you find a compound noun of your own invention, revise, especially when it includes nominalizations. Just reverse the order of words and find prepositions to connect them:

1	2	3	4	5
early	childhood	thought	disorder	misdiagnosis
misdiagnose	disordered	thought	in early	childhood
5	4	3	1	2

Re-assembled:

Physicians misdiagnose[5] disordered[4] thought[3] in young[1] children[2] because they are unfamiliar with recent literature on the subject.

At this point, you may be feeling overwhelmed by all these principles, maybe even wondering whether learning them is worth the effort. Samuel Taylor Coleridge would have thought so, because for him, clarity was a moral issue:

> Whatever is translatable in other and simpler words of the same language, without loss of sense or dignity, is bad.

Cohesion and Coherence

*If he would inform, he must advance regularly from Things known
to things unknown, distinctly without Confusion, and the lower he
begins the better. It is a common Fault in Writers, to allow their
Readers too much knowledge: They begin with that which should
be the Middle, and skipping backwards and forwards, 'tis impossible for any one but he who is perfect in the Subject before, to understand their Work, and such an one has no Occasion to read it.*
—BENJAMIN FRANKLIN

UNDERSTANDING COHERENCE

So far, I've discussed clarity as if we could achieve it just by map-
ping characters and actions onto subjects and verbs. But readers
need more than clear sentences before they think a passage
seems *coherent*. These two passages, for example, say much the
same thing but feel different:

1a. The basis of our American democracy—equal opportunity for
all—is being threatened by college costs that have been rising
fast for the last several years. Increases in family income have
been significantly outpaced by increases in tuition at our
colleges and universities during that period. Only the children
of the wealthiest families in our society will be able to afford a
college education if this trend continues. Knowledge and intellectual skills, in addition to wealth, will divide us as a people,
when that happens. Equal opportunity and the egalitarian basis
of our democratic society could be eroded by such a divide.

✓ 1b. In the last several years, college costs have been rising so fast that they are now threatening the basis of our American democracy—equal opportunity for all. During that period, tuition has significantly outpaced increases in family income. If this trend continues, a college education will soon be affordable only by the children of the wealthiest families in our society. When that happens, we will be divided as a people not only by wealth, but by knowledge and intellectual skills. Such a divide will erode equal opportunity and the egalitarian basis of our democratic society.

The first seems choppy, even disorganized; the second seems to "hang together" better.

But like the word *clarity,* the words *choppy* and *disorganized* refer not to anything on the page, but to how the words on the page make us *feel.* What is it about the *arrangement* of words in (1a) that makes us feel we are moving through it in fits and starts? Why does (1b) seem to flow more easily? We base those judgments on two aspects of word order:

- We judge sequences of sentences to be *cohesive* depending on how each sentence ends and the next begins.

- We judge a whole passage to be *coherent* depending on how all the sentences in a passage cumulatively begin. (In Lesson 6, we discuss two more principles of coherence.)

COHESION

The Sense of Flow

In Lesson 4, we devoted a few pages (48–50) to that familiar advice, *Avoid passives.* If we always did, we would choose the active verb in sentence (2a) below over the passive in (2b):

2a. The collapse of a dead star into a point perhaps no larger than a marble **CREATES**_{active} a black hole.

2b. A black hole **IS CREATED**_{passive} by the collapse of a dead star into a point perhaps no larger than a marble.

But we might choose otherwise if we put those sentences between these two:

> [1]Some astonishing questions about the nature of the universe have been raised by scientists studying black holes in space. [2a/b][————]. [3]So much matter compressed into so little volume changes the fabric of space around it in puzzling ways.

Here's the active sentence there:

> 1a. [1]Some astonishing questions about the nature of the universe have been raised by scientists studying black holes in space. [2a]The collapse of a dead star into a point perhaps no larger than a marble creates a black hole. [3]So much matter compressed into so little volume changes the fabric of space around it in puzzling ways.

And here's the passive:

> 1b. [1]Some astonishing questions about the nature of the universe have been raised by scientists studying black holes in space. [2b]A black hole is created by the collapse of a dead star into a point perhaps no larger than a marble. [3]So much matter compressed into so little volume changes the fabric of space around it in puzzling ways.

Our sense of "flow" calls not for (2a), the sentence with the active verb, but for (2b), the one with the passive.

The reason is clear: the last four words of the first sentence introduce an important character—*black holes in space:*

> [1]Some astonishing questions about the nature of the universe have been raised by scientists studying **black holes in space.**

If we follow it with sentence (2a), the first concepts we hit are collapsed stars and marbles, information that seems to fall from the sky:

> [1]. . . universe have been raised by scientists studying black holes in space. [2a]**The collapse of a dead star into a point perhaps no larger than a marble** creates . . .

But if we follow sentence (1) with (2b), the sentence with the passive verb, we connect those sentences more smoothly, because now the first words in (2b) repeat what we just read at the end of (1):

> [1]. . . studying **black holes in space.** [2b]**A black hole** is created by the collapse of . . .

Note too that the passive also lets us put at the *end* of sentence (2b) words that connect it to the *beginning* of sentence (3):

> [1]. . . black holes in space. [2b]A black hole is created by the collapse of a dead star into **a point perhaps no larger than a marble.** [3]**So much matter compressed into so little volume** changes the fabric of space around it in puzzling ways.

Here's the point: Sentences are cohesive when the last few words of one set up information that appears in the first few words of the next. That gives us our experience of flow. And in fact, that's the biggest reason the passive is in the language: it lets us arrange sentences so that they flow easily from one to the next. We can integrate that insight with our principles about subject and characters, and verbs and actions.

Fixed		
Variable	Familiar	
Fixed	Subject	Verb	————
Variable	Character	Action	————

Diagnosis and Revision

That principle of reading leads us to two principles of revising. They are mirror images of each other. The first is this:

1. **Begin sentences with information familiar to your readers.** Readers get that familiar information from two sources: first, they remember words from the sentence they just read. That's why the beginning of sentence (2b) about black holes coheres with the end of (1) and why the beginning of (3) coheres with the end of (2b):

   > [1]. . . questions about the nature of the universe have been raised by scientists studying **[black holes in space. [2b]A black hole]** is created by the collapse of a dead star into **[a point perhaps no larger than a marble. So much matter compressed into so little volume]** changes the fabric of space . . .

   Second, readers bring to a sentence a general knowledge of its content. We would not be surprised, for example, if a sentence (4) in that paragraph about black holes had begun like this:

   > . . . changes the fabric of space around it in puzzling ways. [4]**Astronomers have reported** that . . .

   The word *Astronomers* did not appear in the preceding sentence, but since we are reading about space, we wouldn't be surprised by a reference to them.

   The second principle is the flip side of the first.

2. **End sentences with information readers cannot predict.** Readers always prefer to read what's hard *after* they read what's easy.

You can more easily see when others fail to observe those principles in their writing than you can in your own, because after you've worked on your own for a while, it all seems familiar— to you. But hard as it is to distinguish old from new in your own mind, you have to try, because readers want to begin sentences with information that is familiar to *them,* and only then move on to information that is new.

> ***Here's the point:***   In every *sequence* of sentences you write, you have to balance principles that make individual sentences clear and principles that make a passage cohesive. *But in that tradeoff, give priority to helping readers create a sense of cohesive flow.* That means starting sentences with information that readers are familiar with. Fortunately, this principle about old and new information cooperates with the principle of characters as subjects. Once you mention your main characters, readers take them as familiar information. So when you regularly get characters up front, you also get up front familiar information.

COHERENCE

The Sense of the Whole

When you create cohesive flow, you take the first step toward helping readers feel that your prose hangs together. But they will judge you to be a competent writer only when they feel that your writing is not just cohesive but *coherent,* a quality different from cohesion. It's easy to confuse the words *cohesion* and *coherence* because they sound alike.

- Think of *cohesion* as pairs of sentences fitting together the way pieces of a jigsaw puzzle do (recall the black hole sentences).

- Think of *coherence* as seeing what all the sentences in a piece of writing add up to, the way all the pieces in a puzzle add up to the picture on the box.

This next passage has good cohesive flow because we move from the end of each sentence to the next without a hitch:

> Sayner, Wisconsin, is the snowmobile capital of the world. The buzzing of snowmobile engines fills the air, and their tanklike tracks crisscross the snow. The snow reminds me of Mom's mashed potatoes, covered with furrows I would draw with my fork. Her mashed potatoes usually make me sick—that's why I play with them. I like to make a hole in the middle of the potatoes and fill it with melted butter. This behavior has been the subject of long chats between me and my analyst.

Though its individual sentences are cohesive, that passage as a whole is incoherent. (It was created by six different writers, one of whom wrote the first sentence, with the other five sequentially adding one sentence, knowing only the immediately preceding one.) It is incoherent for three reasons:

1. The subjects of the sentences are entirely unrelated.
2. The sentences share no common "themes" or ideas.
3. The paragraph has no one sentence that states what the whole passage supports or explains.

Subjects, Topics, Grammar, and Coherence

For five hundred years, English teachers have defined *subject* in two ways:

1. the "doer" of the action
2. what a sentence is "about," its main topic

In Lessons 3 and 4, we saw why that first definition doesn't work: the subjects of many sentences are actions: *The **explosion** was loud.*

But also flawed is that second definition: *A subject is what a sentence is about.* It is flawed because, often, the subject of a sentence doesn't state its main topic, the idea that the rest of the sentence "comments" on. That "topicalizing" function can be performed by other parts of a sentence. For example, none of the main subjects in these sentences name their topics:

- The main subject of this sentence (italicized) is *it*, but the topic of the sentence (boldfaced) is *your claim*, the object of the preposition *for:*

  It is impossible for **your claim** to be proved.

- The subject of this sentence is *I*, but its topic is *this question*, the object of *to:*

  In regard to **this question**, *I* believe more research is needed.

- The subject of this sentence is *it*, but its topic is *our proposal*, the subject of a verb in a subordinate clause:

  It is likely that **our proposal** will be accepted.

- The subject of this sentence is *no one*, but its topic is *such results*, a direct object shifted to the front for emphasis:

  Such results *no one* could have predicted.

Here's the point: We use the term *topic* to mean what a sentence is about, but that topic is not always its grammatical subject. *But readers expect it to be.* They judge writing to be clear and direct when they quickly see topics and subject/characters in the same words.

Diagnosing and Revising Topics

As with other issues of clarity, you can't predict how readers will judge your writing just by reading it, because you know what it means too well. You must analyze it more objectively. This passage feels choppy, out of focus, even disorganized:

> Consistent ideas toward the beginnings of sentences help readers understand what a passage is generally about. A sense of coherence

arises when a sequence of topics comprises a narrow set of related ideas. But the context of each sentence is lost by seemingly random shifts of topics. Unfocused paragraphs result when that happens.

Here's how to diagnose its problems and revise it. You can diagnose and revise your own writing in the same way.

1. **Diagnose**
   a. Underline the first seven or eight words of every sentence in a passage.
   b. If you can, underline the first five or six words of every clause in those sentences, both subordinate and main.

   > <u>Consistent ideas toward the beginnings of sentences, especially in their subjects,</u> help readers understand what a passage is generally about. <u>A sense of coherence</u> arises when a sequence of topics comprises a narrow set of related ideas. But <u>the context of each sentence</u> is lost by seemingly random shifts of topics. <u>Unfocused, even disorganized paragraphs</u> result when that happens.

2. **Analyze**
   a. Are the underlined words a relatively small set of related ideas? Even if *you* see how they are related, will your readers? For that passage, the answer is no.
   b. Do those words name the most important characters, real or abstract? Again, the answer is no.

3. **Rewrite**
   a. In most (not necessarily all) of your sentences, use subjects to name their topics.
   b. Be sure that those topics are, in context, familiar information to your readers.

Here is that passage revised, with the new topics boldfaced.

> **Readers** understand what a passage is generally about when **they** see consistent ideas toward the beginnings of sentences, especially in their subjects. **They** feel a passage is coherent when **they** read a sequence of topics that focuses on a narrow set of related ideas.

But when topics seem to shift randomly, **readers** lose the context of each sentence. When **that** happens, **they** feel they are reading paragraphs that are unfocused and even disorganized.

THE DIFFICULT CRAFT OF BEGINNING A SENTENCE WELL

It's hard to begin a sentence well. Readers want to get to topic/subjects quickly, but too often, we begin sentences in ways that keep readers from getting there. It's called *throat-clearing*. Throat-clearing typically begins with metadiscourse (review pp. 51–53) that connects a sentence to the previous one. These include common transitions such as *and, but, therefore:*

> And therefore . . .

We then add a second kind of metadiscourse that expresses our attitude toward what is coming, words such as *fortunately, perhaps, allegedly, it is important to note, for the most part,* or *politically speaking:*

> And therefore, it is important to note . . .

Then we indicate time, place, or manner:

> And therefore, it is important to note that, in eastern states since 1980 . . .

Only then do we get to the topic/subject:

> And, therefore, it is important to note that, in eastern states since 1980, **acid rain** has become a serious problem.

When you open several sentences like that, your readers have a hard time seeing not just what each sentence is about, but the focus of a whole passage. When you find a sentence with lots of words before its subject/topic, revise:

> ✓ Since 1980, therefore, **acid rain** has become a political problem in the eastern states.

> ***Here's the point:***   In most of your sentences (not necessarily all), start with the subject and make that subject the topic of the sentence.

INTEGRATING THE PRINCIPLES

We can bring together these principles about old and new and strings of consistent topics with the principles about characters as subjects and actions as verbs (I'll fill in the empty boxes in Lesson 6):

Fixed	Topic		
Variable	Familiar, short		
Fixed	Subject	Verb	————
Variable	Character	Action	————

Learning to write clear sentences is hard enough. Even more demanding is assembling those sentences into a passage that is both cohesive and coherent. The nineteenth century essayist Thomas De Quincey understood its importance:

> The two capital secrets in the art of prose composition are these: first the philosophy of translation and connection; . . . all fluent and effective composition depends on the connections; secondly, the way in which sentences are made to modify each other; for the most powerful effects in which eloquence arise out of this reverberation, as it were, from each other in a rapid succession of sentences.

6

Emphasis

In the end is my beginning.
—T. S. ELIOT

UNDERSTANDING HOW SENTENCES END

If you consistently write sentences whose subject/topics name a few central characters and join them to strong verbs, you'll likely get the rest of the sentence right, and in the process create a passage that is both cohesive and coherent. But if the first few words of a sentence are worth special attention, so are the last few, because how you end a sentence determines how readers judge both its clarity and its strength. In this lesson, we address clarity first, then strength, then how the right emphasis on the right words can contribute to a kind of coherence even more global than the coherence we get from consistent topics.

When readers can build up momentum in the first nine or ten words of a sentence, the more easily they get through complicated material that follows. Compare:

1a. A sociometric and actuarial analysis of Social Security revenues and disbursements for the last six decades to determine changes in projecting deficits is the subject of this study.

✓1b. In this study, we analyze Social Security's revenues and disbursements for the last six decades, using sociometric and actuarial criteria to determine changes in projecting deficits.

As we start (1a), we struggle to understand its technical terms at the same time we are hacking through a subject twenty-two words long. In (1b), we go through just five words to get past a subject and verb and twelve more before we hit a term that might slow us up. By that point we have enough momentum to carry us through the complexity to its end. In short, in (1a), we hit the complexity at the beginning; in (1b), we don't hit it until near the end, where we can handle it better.

There are, however, two kinds of complexity: grammar and meaning.

Complex Grammar

Which of these two sentences do you prefer?

> 2a. Lincoln's claim that the Civil War was God's punishment of both North and South for slavery appears in the last part of the speech.
>
> 2b. In the last part of his speech, Lincoln claims that God gave the Civil War to both North and South as a punishment for slavery.

Most readers prefer (2b), because it begins simply with a short introductory phrase followed by a one-word subject and a specific verb, then moves toward grammatical complexity. We discussed that issue in Lesson 5.

Complex Meaning

Another kind of complexity is in the meanings of words. Readers have a problem with new technical terms, but especially at the beginning of a sentence. Compare these two passages:

> 3a. The role of calcium blocker drugs in the control of cardiac irregularity can be seen through an understanding of the role of calcium in the activation of muscle cells. The regulatory proteins actin, myosin, tropomyosin, and troponin make up the sarcomere, the basic unit of muscle contraction. ATPase, the energy-

producing protein myosin, makes up its thick filament, while actin, tropomyosin, and troponin make up its thin filament. Interaction of myosin and actin triggers muscle contraction.

✓3b. When a muscle contracts, it uses calcium. We must therefore understand how calcium affects muscle cells to understand how cardiac irregularity is controlled by drugs called "calcium blockers." The basic unit of muscle contraction is the sarcomere. It has two filaments, one thin and one thick. Those filaments consist of four proteins that regulate contraction: actin, myosin, tropomyosin, and troponin. Muscles contract when the protein in the thin filament, actin, interacts with the protein myosin in the thick filament, an energy-producing or ATPase protein.

Both passages use the same technical terms, but (3b) is clearer to those who know nothing about the chemistry of muscles.

Those passages differ in two ways. First, information that is only implicit in (3a) is explicit in (3b):

3a. . . . and troponin make up the sarcomere, the basic unit of muscle contraction. ATPase, the energy-producing protein myosin, makes up its thick filament.

✓3b. The basic unit of muscle contraction is the sarcomere. It has two filaments, one thin and one thick . . .

More important, note how almost all the technical terms in (3a) are toward the beginnings of their sentences and, the familiar ones are toward the end:

3a. The role of **calcium blocker drugs** in the control of **cardiac irregularity** can be seen through an understanding of the role of calcium in the activation of muscle cells.

The regulatory proteins actin, myosin, tropomyosin, and troponin make up the **sarcomere,** the basic unit of muscle contraction.

ATPase, the energy-producing protein myosin, makes up its thick filament, while **actin, tropomyosin, and troponin** make up its thin filament.

Interaction of myosin and actin triggers muscle contraction.

In (3b), I moved those technical terms to the ends of their sentences:

> . . . uses **calcium.**

> . . . controlled by drugs called **"calcium blockers."**

> . . . is the **sarcomere.**

> . . . four proteins that regulate contraction: **actin, myosin, tropomyosin, and troponin.**

> . . . in the thick filament, an **energy-producing or ATPase protein.**

These principles work for prose intended even for professional readers. In this next passage from the *New England Journal of Medicine*, the writer deliberately uses metadiscourse just to put a new technical term at its end:

> The incubation of peripheral-blood lymphocytes with a lymphokine, interleukin-2, generates lymphoid cells that can lyse fresh, noncultured, natural-killer-cell-resistant tumor cells but not normal cells. *We term these cells* **lymphokine-activated killer (LAK) cells.**

Here's the point: Your readers want you to use the end of your sentences to help them manage two kinds of difficulty:

- long and complex phrases and clauses,
- new information, particularly unfamiliar technical terms.

In general, begin your sentences with elements that are relatively short: short introductory phrases and clauses, followed by a short, concrete subject, followed by a verb expressing a specific action. After the verb, the sentence can go on for several lines, if it is well constructed (see Lesson 8). The general principle is to carry the reader from simplicity to complexity. We can integrate that principle with our others:

Fixed	Topic		
Variable	Short, simple, familiar	⋮	New, long, complex
Fixed	Subject	Verb	———
Variable	Character	Action	———

ONE MORE NEW TERM: *STRESS*

In the last lesson, we said that an important position in the *psychological* geography of a sentence is its first few words, because they name the topic of a sentence, its *psychological* as opposed to its grammatical subject (see pp. 61–62). In this lesson, I've discussed the end of a sentence in general, but its last two or three words are particularly important. You can sense that when at the end of sentence you hear your voice rise and emphasize one syllable more strongly than you do the others:

. . . more strongly than you do the ^{6}-thers.

We have the same experience when reading silently.

We'll call this most emphatic part of a sentence its *stress* and add it to our last box. How you manage the emphasis in that stress position helps establish the voice readers hear in your prose, because if you end a sentence on light words that carry little meaning, your sentence will seem to end weakly.

> Global warming could raise sea levels to a point where much of the world's low-lying coastal areas would disappear, **according to most atmospheric scientists.**

✓ According to most atmospheric scientists, global warming could raise sea levels to a point where much of the world's low-lying coastal areas **would disappear.**

Fixed	Topic		Stress
Variable	Short, simple, familiar		New, long, complex
Fixed	Subject	Verb	————
Variable	Character	Action	————

In Lesson 4, we saw how to use different subjects to begin a sentence from different points of view (pp. 49–50). You can also create different stylistic effects by managing how your sentences end.

Compare these next passages. One was written to blame an American president for being weak with Iran on arms control. The other is a revision that stresses Iran. The ends of the sentences tell you which is which:

1a. The administration has blurred an issue central to nuclear arms control, **the issue of verification.** Irresponsible charges, innuendo, and leaks have submerged **serious problems with Iranian compliance.** The objective, instead, should be not to exploit these concerns in order to further poison our relations, repudiate existing agreements, or, worse still, terminate arms control altogether, but to **insist on compliance and clarify questionable behavior.**

1b. The issue of verification—so central to arms control—has been **blurred by the administration.** Serious problems with Iranian compliance have been submerged in **irresponsible charges, innuendo, and leaks.** The objective, instead, should be to clarify questionable behavior and insist on compliance—not to exploit these concerns in order to **further poison our relations, repudiate existing agreements, or, worse still, terminate arms control altogether.**

> ***Here's the point:*** Just as you look at the first few
> words of your sentences for point of view, look at the last
> few words for special emphasis. You can revise a sentence
> to emphasize particular words that you want readers to
> hear stressed and thereby note as particularly significant.

DIAGNOSIS AND REVISION

If you have managed your subjects and topics well, you will by
default move the words you want to emphasize toward the ends
of your sentences. But you might still not end them on quite the
right words. To test whether you've done this, read your sentence aloud, and as you reach the last three or four words, tap
your finger hard as if emphasizing them in a speech. If you tap
on words that do not seem to deserve strong emphasis, look for
words that do, then rewrite the sentence to get those words
closer to the end. Here are some ways to do that.

Three Tactical Revisions

1. **Trim the end.**

   Sociobiologists claim that our genes control our social behavior **in the way we act in situations we are in every day.**

   Since *social behavior* means *the way we act in situations . . . ,*
   we drop everything after *behavior:*

   ✓ Sociobiologists claim that our genes **control our social behavior.**

2. **Shift peripheral ideas to the left.**

   The data offered to prove ESP are weak, **for the most part.**

   ✓ **For the most part,** the data offered to prove ESP are **weak.**

   Particularly avoid ending with anticlimactic metadiscourse:

   Job opportunities in computer programming are getting scarcer,
   it must be remembered.

✓ **It must be remembered** that job opportunities in computer programming are getting scarcer.

3. **Shift new information to the right.**
A more common way to manage stress is by moving new information to the end of a sentence.

> **Questions about the ethics of withdrawing intravenous feeding** are *more difficult [than something just mentioned].*

> ✓ *More difficult [than something just mentioned]* are **questions about the ethics of withdrawing intravenous feeding.**

Six Syntactic Devices to Emphasize the Right Words

There are several syntactic devices that let you manage where in a sentence you stress units of new information. You just read one of them.

1. ***There***   Some editors discourage all *there is/there are* constructions, but a *there* lets you shift a subject to the right, thereby emphasizing it. Compare:

> **Several syntactic devices** let you manage where in a sentence you locate units of new information.

> ✓ *There are* **several syntactic devices** that let you manage where in a sentence you locate units of new information.

Experienced writers commonly begin a paragraph with *there* to introduce new topics and concepts that they develop in what follows.

2. **Passives (for the last time)**   A passive verb lets you flip a subject and object. Compare these next two sentences:

> Some claim that **our genes** influence$_{active}$ aspects of behavior that we think are learned. **Our genes,** for example, seem to determine . . .

> ✓ Some claim that aspects of behavior that we think are learned are in fact influenced$_{passive}$ **by our genes. Our genes,** for example, seem to determine . . .

To stress the concept of genes influencing behavior, I revised the active verb into a passive to get that idea into the stress position. The passive is in the language so that we can get old and new information in the right order.

3. ***What* shift**   This is another device that shifts a part of the sentence to the right, thereby emphasizing it more:

> We need a monetary policy that would end fluctuations in money supply, unemployment, and inflation.

> ✓ **What** we need **is** a monetary policy that would end fluctuations in money supply, unemployment, and inflation.

4. ***It* shift**   When you have a subject consisting of a long noun clause, you can move it to the end of the sentence and start with an *it:*

> **That oil prices would be set by OPEC** once seemed inevitable.

> ✓ *It* once seemed inevitable **that oil prices would be set by OPEC.**

5. ***Not only X, but Y (as well)***   In this next pair, note how the *but* emphasizes the last element of the pair:

> We must clarify these issues **and develop deeper trust.**

> ✓ We must *not only* clarify these issues, *but* **develop deeper trust.**

Unless you have reason to emphasize the negative, end with the positive:

> The point is to highlight our success, **not to emphasize our failures.**

> ✓ The point is not to emphasize our failures, but **to highlight our success.**

The cost of these five devices is a few extra words, so use them sparingly.

6. **Pronoun substitution, and ellipsis** This is a fine point: a sentence can end flatly when you repeat a word that you used just a few words before at the end of a sentence, because the voice we hear in our mind's ear drops off at the end. If you read aloud the preceding sentence, this one, and the next, you can hear that drop at the end of each sentence. To avoid that kind of flatness, rewrite or use a pronoun instead of repeating the word at the end of the sentence. For example:

> A sentence will seem to end flatly if at its end you use a word that you used just a few words before, because when you repeat that word, your voice **drops.** Instead of repeating the noun, use a **pronoun.** The reader will at least hear emphasis on the word just **before** *it*.

Occasionally, you can just delete words that repeat earlier ones:

> It is sometimes possible to represent a complex idea in a simple sentence, but more often you cannot.

One of the characteristics of especially elegant prose is how writers use a handful of rhetorical figures to end their sentences. I will discuss those devices in Lesson 9.

TOPICS, EMPHASIS, THEMES, AND COHERENCE

There is one more function performed by the stress of certain sentences, one that helps readers think a whole passage is coherent. As we saw in the last lesson, readers take the clearest topic to be a short noun phrase that comes early in a sentence, usually as its subject. That's why most of us judge this next paragraph to be unfocused: its sentences seem to open randomly, from no consistent point of view:

1a. Great strides in the early and accurate diagnosis of Alzheimer's disease have been made in recent years. Not too long ago, senility in an older patient who seemed to be losing touch with reality was often confused with Alzheimer's. Genetic clues have become the basis of newer and more reliable tests in the last few years, however. The risk of human tragedy of another kind, though, has resulted from the increasing accuracy of these tests: predictions about susceptibility to Alzheimer's have become possible, long before the appearance of any overt symptoms. At that point, an apparently healthy person could be devastated by such an early diagnosis.

If we revise that passage to make the topics more consistent, we also make it more coherent (topics are boldfaced):

✓1b. In recent years, **researchers** have made great strides in the early and accurate diagnosis of Alzheimer's disease. Not too long ago, when a **physician** examined an older patient who seemed out of touch with reality, **she had** to guess whether the **person** was senile or had Alzheimer's. In the past few years, however, **physicians** have been able to use new and more reliable tests focusing on genetic clues. But in **the accuracy of these new tests** lies the risk of another kind of human tragedy: **physicians** may be able to predict Alzheimer's long before its overt appearance, but **such an early diagnosis** could psychologically devastate an apparently healthy person.

The passage now focuses on just two topics: researcher/physicians and testing/diagnosis.

But there is one more revision that would make that passage even more of a whole:

Put key words in the stress position of the *first* sentence of a passage to emphasize the key ideas in the rest of it.

The first sentence of that paragraph now stresses advances in diagnosis: . . . *the early and accurate diagnosis of Alzheimer's disease.* But the point in this passage is not about diagnosis, but about its risks. That concept, however, does not appear until we are more than halfway through that paragraph.

Readers would grasp the point of that passage better if all of its key concepts appeared in the first sentence, and (here is where it gets detailed) *specifically toward its end, in its stress position.* Readers read the opening sentence or two of a paragraph to find the key concepts that the paragraph will repeat and develop, *and they specifically look for those concepts in the last few words of those opening, introductory, framing sentences.*

Here is a new first sentence for the Alzheimer's paragraph that would help readers focus on the key concepts not just of *Alzheimer's* and *new diagnoses,* but of *new problem* and *informing those most at risk.*

> In recent years, researchers have made great strides in the early and accurate diagnosis of Alzheimer's disease, but those **diagnoses** have raised **a new problem** about **informing those most at risk who show no symptoms of it.**

We can call those key concepts that run through a passage its *themes.*

Look at the highlighted words in the passage below one more time:

- The boldfaced words are about testing.
- The italicized words are about mental states.
- The capitalized words are about a new problem.

Each of those concepts is announced toward the end of a new opening sentence, especially the theme of the new problem.

✓ 1c. In recent years, researchers have made great strides in the early and accurate **diagnosis** of *Alzheimer's disease,* but those **diagnoses** have raised A NEW PROBLEM about INFORMING THOSE *MOST AT RISK* WHO SHOW *NO SYMPTOMS OF IT.* Not too long ago, when a physician examined an older patient who seemed *out of touch with reality,* she had to **guess** whether that person had *Alzheimer's* or was *only senile.* In the past few years, however, physicians have been able to use **new and more reliable tests** focusing on genetic clues. But in the accuracy of these **new tests** lies the RISK OF ANOTHER KIND OF HUMAN TRAGEDY: physicians may be able to **predict** *Alzheimer's* long before its overt appearance, but such an early **diagnosis** could PSYCHOLOGICALLY DEVASTATE AN APPARENTLY HEALTHY PERSON.

That passage now "hangs together" not for just one reason, but for three:

- Its topics consistently focus on physicians and diagnosis.
- Running through it are strings of words that focus on the themes of (1) tests, (2) mental conditions, and (3) a new problem.
- *And no less important, the opening sentence helps us notice those themes by emphasizing them at its end.*

This principle applies to sentences that introduce fairly long paragraphs (two or three-sentence introductory, transitional, and other kinds of paragraphs follow different patterns). It also applies to sentences that introduce passages of any length, even to a whole document.

Here's the point: We depend on concepts running through a passage to create a sense of its coherence. You help readers identify those concepts in two ways:

- Repeat some of them as topics of sentences, usually as subjects.
- Repeat others as themes elsewhere in a passage, in nouns, verbs, and adjectives.

Readers are more likely to notice those themes if you emphasize them at the end of the sentence that introduces that passage.

There is an old German proverb that captures this principle quite nicely:

Beginning and end shake hands with one another.

Concision

To a Snail: If "compression is the first grace of style,"
you have it.
—MARIANNE MOORE

CLARITY, GRACE, AND CONCISION

You get close to clarity when you match your character and actions to your subjects and verbs, and closer yet when you get the right characters into topics and the right words under stress. But readers may still think your prose is a long way from graceful if it's anything like this:

> In my personal opinion, it is necessary that we should not ignore the opportunity to think over each and every suggestion offered.

That writer matched characters with subjects, and actions with verbs, but in too many words: opinion is always personal, so we don't need *personal*, and since this statement is opinion, we don't need *in my opinion*. *Think over* and *not ignore* both mean *consider*. *Each and every* is redundant. A suggestion is by definition offered. In fewer words:

✓ We should consider each suggestion.

Though not elegant, that sentence at least has style's first grace—compression, or as we'll call it, *concision*. Concision, though, is only a start. You must still make your sentences shapely. In this lesson, I focus on concision; in the next, on shape.

DIAGNOSIS AND REVISION

Six Principles of Concision

When I edited that sentence about suggestions, I followed six principles:

1. Delete words that mean little or nothing.
2. Delete words that repeat the meaning of other words.
3. Delete words implied by other words.
4. Replace a phrase with a word.
5. Change negatives to affirmatives.
6. Delete useless adjectives and adverbs

Those principles are easy to state but hard to follow, because you have to inch your way through every sentence you write, cutting here, compressing there, and that's labor intensive. Those six principles, though, can guide you in that work.

1. Delete Meaningless Words   Some words are verbal tics that we use as unconsciously as we clear our throats:

kind of	actually	particular	really	certain	various
virtually	individual	basically	generally	given	practically

Productivity **actually** depends on **certain** factors that **basically** involve psychology more than **any particular** technology.

✓ Productivity depends on psychology more than on technology.

2. Delete Doubled Words   Early in the history of English, writers got into the habit pairing a French or Latin word with a native English one, because foreign words sounded more learned. Most paired words today are just redundant. Among the common ones:

full and complete	hope and trust	any and all
true and accurate	each and every	basic and fundamental
hope and desire	first and foremost	various and sundry

3. Delete What Readers Can Infer   This redundancy is common but hard to identify, because it comes in so many forms.

Redundant Modifiers   Often, the meaning of a word implies its modifier:

> Do not try to *predict* those **future** events that will **completely** *revolutionize* society, because **past** *history* shows that it is the **final** *outcome* of minor events that **unexpectedly** *surprises* us more.

✓ Do not try to predict revolutionary events, because history shows that the outcome of minor events surprises us more.

Some common redundancies:

terrible tragedy	various different	free gift
basic fundamentals	future plans	each individual
final outcome	true facts	consensus of opinion

Redundant Categories   Every word implies its general category, so you can usually cut a word that names it. Compare (the category is boldfaced):

> During that *period* **of time,** the *membrane* **area** became *pink* **in color** and *shiny* **in appearance.**

✓ During that *period*, the *membrane* became *pink* and *shiny*.

In doing that, you may have to change an adjective into an adverb:

> The holes must be aligned in an *accurate* **manner.**

✓ The holes must be aligned *accurately*.

Sometimes you change an adjective into a noun:

> The county manages the *educational* **system** and *public recreational* **activities.**

✓ The county manages *education* and *public recreation*.

Here are some general nouns (boldfaced) often used redundantly:

large in **size**	round in **shape**	honest in **character**
unusual in **nature**	of a strange **type**	**area** of mathematics
of a bright **color**	at an early **time**	in a confused **state**

General Implications This kind of wordiness is even harder to spot, because it can be so diffuse:

> Imagine someone trying to learn the rules for playing the game of chess.

Learn implies *trying, playing the game* implies *rules*, chess is a game. So more concisely,

> Imagine learning the rules of chess.

4. Replace a Phrase with a Word This redundancy is especially difficult to fix, because you need a big vocabulary and the wit to use it. For example:

> As you carefully read what you have written to improve wording and catch errors of spelling and punctuation, the thing to do before anything else is to see whether you can use sequences of subjects and verbs instead of the same ideas expressed in nouns.

That is,

> ✓ As you edit, first replace nominalizations with clauses.

I compressed five phrases into five words:

carefully read what you have written	→	edit
the thing to do before anything else	→	first
use X instead of Y	→	replace
nouns instead of verbs	→	nominalizations
sequences of subjects and verbs	→	clauses

I can offer no principle that tells you what phrases to replace with a word, much less give you the word. I can point out only that you often can, and that you should be alert for opportunities to do so—which is to say, try.

Here are some common phrases (boldfaced) to watch for. Note that some of them let you turn a nominalization into a verb (both italicized):

> We must explain **the reason for** the *delay* in the meeting.
> ✓ We must explain **why** the meeting is *delayed*.

Despite the fact that the data were checked, errors occurred.
✓ **Even though** the data were checked, errors occurred.

In the event that you finish early, contact this office.
✓ **If** you finish early, contact this office.

In a situation where a class closes, you may petition to get in.
✓ **When** a class closes, you may petition to get in.

I want to say a few words **concerning the matter of** money.
✓ I want to say a few words **about** money.

There is a need for more careful *inspection* of all welds.
✓ You **must** *inspect* all welds more carefully.

We **are in a position** to make you an offer.
✓ We **can** make you an offer.

It is possible that nothing will come of this.
✓ Nothing **may** come of this.

Prior to the *end* of the training, apply for your license.
✓ **Before** training *ends,* apply for your license.

We have noted a **decrease/increase in** the number of errors.
✓ We have noted *fewer/more* errors.

5. Change Negatives to Affirmatives   When you express an
idea in a negative form, not only must you use an extra word:
same → *not different,* but you also force readers to do a kind of
algebraic calculation. These two sentences, for example, mean
much the same thing, but the affirmative is more direct:

Do not write in the negative. → Write in the affirmative.

You can rewrite most negatives, some formulaically:

not careful	→	careless	not many	→	few
not the same	→	different	not often	→	rarely
not allow	→	prevent	not stop	→	continue
not notice	→	overlook	not include	→	omit

Do not translate a negative into an affirmative if you want to emphasize the negative. (Is that such a sentence? I could have written, *Keep a negative sentence when . . .*)

Some verbs, prepositions, and conjunctions are implicitly negative:

Verbs	*preclude, prevent, lack, fail, doubt, reject, avoid, deny, refuse, exclude, contradict, prohibit, bar*
Prepositions	*without, against, lacking, but for, except*
Conjunctions	*unless, except when*

You can baffle readers if you combine *not* with these negative words. Compare these:

> **Except** when you have **failed** to submit applications **without** documentation, benefits will **not** be **denied.**

✓ You will receive benefits only if you submit your documents.

✓ To receive benefits, submit your documents.

And you baffle readers completely when you combine explicitly and implicitly negative words with passives and nominalizations:

> There should be **no** submission of payments **without** notification of this office, **unless** the payment does **not** exceed $100.

> Do not **submit** payments if you have not **notified** this office, unless you are **paying** less than $100.

Now revise the negatives into affirmatives:

✓ If you pay more than $100, notify this office first.

6. Delete Adjectives and Adverbs   Many writers can't resist adding useless adjectives and adverbs. Try deleting every adverb and every adjective before a noun, then restore *only* those that readers need to understand the passage. In this passage, which ones should be restored?

> At the heart of the argument culture is our habit of seeing issues and ideas as ~~absolute and irreconcilable~~ principles ~~continually~~ at

war. To move beyond this ~~static and limiting~~ view, we can remember the ~~Chinese~~ approach to yin and yang. They are ~~two~~ principles, yes, but they are conceived not as ~~irreconcilable polar~~ opposites but as elements that coexist and should be brought into balance ~~as much as possible~~. As sociolinguist Suzanne Wong Scollon notes, "Yin is always present in and changing into yang and vice versa." How can we translate this ~~abstract~~ idea into ~~daily~~ practice?

—Deborah Tannen, *The Argument Culture*

Here's the point: Readers think you write concisely when you use only enough words to say what you mean.

1. Delete words that mean little or nothing.
2. Delete words that repeat the meaning of other words.
3. Delete words implied by other words.
4. Replace a phrase with a word.
5. Change negatives to affirmatives.
6. Delete useless adjectives and adverbs.

A PARTICULAR KIND OF REDUNDANCY: METADISCOURSE

Lesson 4 described metadiscourse as language that refers to the following:

- the writer's intentions: *to sum up, candidly, I believe*
- directions to the reader: *note that, consider now, as you see*
- the structure of the text: *first, second, finally, therefore, however*

Everything you write needs metadiscourse, but too much buries your ideas:

> The last point I would like to make is that in regard to men-women relationships, it is important to keep in mind that the greatest changes have occurred in how they work together.

Only nine of those thirty-four words address men-women relationships:

> men-women relationships . . . greatest changes . . . how they work together.

The rest is metadiscourse:

> The last point I would like to make is that in regard to . . . it is important to keep in mind that . . .

When we prune the metadiscourse, we tighten the sentence:

> The greatest changes in men-women relationships have occurred in how they work together.

Now that we see what the sentence says, we can make it still more direct:

> ✓ Men and women have changed their relationships most in how they work together.

Some teachers and editors urge us to cut all metadiscourse, but everything we write needs some. You have to read with an eye to how good writers in your field use it, then do likewise.

There are, however, some types that you can usually cut.

Metadiscourse That Attributes Your Ideas to a Source Don't announce that something has been *observed, noticed, noted,* and so on; just state the fact:

> High divorce rates **have been observed** to occur in areas that **have been determined to have** low population density.

> ✓ High divorce rates occur in areas with low population density.

Metadiscourse That Announces Your Topic The boldface phrases tell your reader what your sentence is "about":

> **This section introduces another** problem, that of noise pollution. **The first thing to say about it is** that noise pollution exists not only . . .

Readers catch the topic more easily if you reduce the metadiscourse:

> ✓ **Another** problem is noise pollution. **First,** it exists not only . . .

Two other constructions call attention to a topic, usually one already mentioned in the text:

> **In regard to** a vigorous style, the most important feature is a short, concrete subject followed by a forceful verb.
>
> **So far as** China's industrial development **is concerned,** it will take only a few years to equal that of Japan.

But you can usually work those topics into a subject:

> ✓ **The most important feature of a vigorous style** is a short, concrete subject followed by a forceful verb.
>
> ✓ **China** will take only a few years to equal Japan's industrial development.

Look hard at a sentence opening with a metadiscourse subject and verb that merely announce a topic:

> In this essay, **I will discuss** the role of metaphor in style.

I write that kind of sentence when I have no idea where I am going, saying in effect, *I have this topic and hope I eventually think of something to say about it.* On the other hand, that kind of sentence in a professional journal promises to develop what it names.

Metadiscourse That Hedges and Intensifies   Another kind of metadiscourse reflects the writer's certainty about what she is claiming. This kind of metadiscourse comes in two flavors, *hedges* and *intensifiers.* Hedges qualify your certainty; intensifiers increase it. Both can not only be redundant, but influence how readers judge your character, because they signal how well you balance caution and confidence.

> *Hedges*   These are common hedges:
>
> **Adverbs**   *usually, often, sometimes, almost, virtually, possibly, allegedly, arguably, perhaps, apparently, in some ways, to a certain extent, somewhat, in some/certain respects*

Adjectives	*most, many, some, a certain number of*
Verbs	*may, might, can, could, seem, tend, appear, suggest, indicate*

Some readers think all hedging is not just redundant, but mealy-mouthed:

> There **seems to be some** evidence to **suggest** that **certain** differences between Japanese and Western rhetoric **could** derive from historical influences **possibly** traceable to Japan's cultural isolation and Europe's history of cross-cultural contacts.

On the other hand, only a fool or someone with vast historical evidence would make a claim as confident as this:

> This evidence **proves** that Japanese and Western rhetorics differ because of Japan's cultural isolation and Europe's history of cross-cultural contacts.

In most academic writing, we more often state claims closer to this (and look at that for my own hedging; compare the more assertive, *In academic writing, we state claims like this*):

> ✓ This evidence **suggests** that **aspects** of Japanese and Western rhetoric differ because of Japan's cultural isolation and Europe's history of cross-cultural contacts.

The verbs *suggest* and *indicate* let you state a claim about which you are less than 100 percent certain, but confident enough to propose:

> ✓ The evidence **indicates** that some of these questions remain unresolved.
> ✓ These data **suggest** that further studies are necessary.

Even confident scientists hedge. This next paragraph introduced the most significant breakthrough in the history of genetics, the discovery of the double helix of DNA. If anyone was entitled to be assertive, it was Crick and Watson. But they chose to be diffident (note, too, the first-person *we;* hedges are boldfaced):

We **wish to suggest a** [not *the*] structure for the salt of deoxyribose nucleic acid (D.N.A.) . . . A structure for nucleic acid has already been proposed by Pauling and Corey . . . **In our opinion,** this structure is unsatisfactory for two reasons: (1) **We believe** that the material which gives the X-ray diagrams is the salt, not the free acid . . . (2) **Some** of the van der Waals distances **appear** to be too small.

> —J. D. Watson and F. H. C. Crick,
> "Molecular Structure of Nucleic Acids"

Without the hedges, their claim would be more concise but more aggressive. Compare this (I boldface my stronger words, but most of the more aggressive tone comes from the absence of hedges):

We ~~wish to suggest~~ **state here a the** structure for the salt of deoxyribose nucleic acid (D.N.A.) . . . A structure for nucleic acid has already been proposed by Pauling and Corey . . . ~~In our opinion,~~ [T]his structure is unsatisfactory for two reasons: (1) ~~We believe that~~ [T]he material which gives the X-ray diagrams is the salt, not the free acid . . . (2) ~~Some of~~ [T]he van der Waals distances ~~appear to be~~ **are** too small.

Intensifiers   These are common intensifiers:

Adverbs	*very, pretty, quite, rather, clearly, obviously, undoubtedly, certainly, of course, indeed, inevitably, invariably, always*
Adjectives	*key, central, crucial, basic, fundamental, major, principal, essential*
Verbs	*show, prove, establish, as you/we/everyone knows/can see, it is clear/obvious that*

The most common intensifier is the absence of a hedge. In this case, less is more. The first sentence below has no intensifiers at the blanks, but neither does it have any hedges, and so it seems like a strong claim:

_____ Americans believe that the federal government is _____ intrusive and _____ authoritarian.

✓ **Many** Americans believe that the federal government is **often** intrusive and **increasingly** authoritarian.

Confident writers use intensifiers less often than they use hedges because they want to avoid sounding as assertive as this:

> For a century now, **all** liberals have argued against **any** censorship of art, and **every** court has found their arguments so **completely** persuasive that **not a** person **any** longer remembers how they were countered. As a result, today, censorship is **totally** a thing of the past.

Some writers think that kind of aggressive style is persuasive. Quite the opposite: if you state a claim moderately, readers are more likely to consider it thoughtfully:

> For **about** a century now, **many** liberals have argued against censorship of art, and **most** courts have found their arguments persuasive **enough** that **few** people **may** remember **exactly** how they were countered. As a result, today, censorship is **virtually** a thing of the past.

Some claim that a passage hedged that much is wordy and weak. Perhaps. But it does not come on like a bulldozer. It leaves room for a reasoned and equally moderate response.

Here's the point: You need some metadiscourse in everything you write, especially metadiscourse that guides readers through your text, words such as *first, second, therefore, on the other hand,* and so on. You also need some metadiscourse that hedges your certainty, words such as *perhaps, seems, could,* and so on. The risk is in using too many.

For the best writers, a concern with style always begins by thinking about readers. That's what motivated the founder of the Methodist church, John Wesley:

> I write for those who judge of books, not by the quantity, but by the quality of them: who ask not how long, but how good they are? I spare both my reader's time and my own, by couching my sense in as few words as I can.

Lesson

8

Shape

*Sentences in their variety run from simplicity to complexity,
a progression not necessarily reflected in length: a long sentence
may be extremely simple in construction—indeed must be simple
if it is to convey its sense easily.*
—SIR HERBERT READ

UNDERSTANDING THE SHAPE OF SENTENCES

If you can write clear and concise sentences, you have achieved
a good deal, and more if you can assemble them into coherent
passages. But if you couldn't write a clear sentence longer than
twenty words or so, you'd be like a composer who could write
only jingles. Some advise against long sentences, but you cannot communicate every complex idea in a short one: you have
to know how to write a sentence that is both long and clear.

Consider, for example, this sentence:

> In addition to differences in religion that have for centuries
> plagued Sunnis and Shiites, explanations of the causes of their dis-
> trust must include all of the other social, economic, and cultural
> conflicts that have plagued them that are rooted in a troubled his-
> tory that extends 1,300 years into the past.

Even if that idea needed all those words (it doesn't), they could
be arranged into a more shapely sentence.

We can start revising by editing the abstractions into char-acter/subjects and action/verbs and then break the sentence into shorter ones:

> Historians have tried to explain why Sunnis and Shiites distrust one another today. Many have claimed that the sources of conflict are age-old differences in religion. But they must study all the other social, economic, and cultural conflicts that have plagued their 1,300 years of troubled history.

But that passage feels choppy. We prefer something like this:

> ✓ To explain why Sunnis and Shiites distrust one another today, his-torians must study not only age-old religious differences, but all the other social, economic, and cultural conflicts that have plagued their 1,300 years of troubled history.

That sentence is thirty-six words long, but it doesn't sprawl. So it can't be length alone that makes a sentence ungainly. In this lesson, I focus on how to write sentences that are not only long and complex but clear and shapely.

DIAGNOSIS AND REVISION

As with other issues of style, you can see sprawl in the writing of others more easily than you can in your own, so you have to diagnose your prose in ways that sidestep your intractable subjectivity.

Start by putting a slash mark after every period and ques-tion mark./Then pick out sentences longer than two lines and read them aloud./If in reading one of your long sentences you feel that you are about to run out of breath before you come to a place where you can pause to integrate all of its parts into a whole that communicates a single conceptual structure [breathe], you have found a sentence, like this one, that your readers would likely want you to revise./Or if your sentence, be-cause of one interruption after another, seems to stop and start, your readers are, if they are typical, likely to judge that your sen-tence, as this one does, lurches from one part to the next.

Readers get a sense of shapeless length from three things:

- It takes readers too long to get to the verb in the main clause.
- After the verb, they have to slog through a shapeless sprawl of tacked-on subordinate clauses.
- They stumble over one interruption after another.

Revising Long Openings

Some sentences seem to take forever to get started:

> Since most undergraduate students change their fields of study at least once during their college careers, many more than once, first-year students who are not certain about their program of studies should not load up their schedules to meet requirements for a particular program.

That sentence takes thirty-one words to get to its main verb, *should not load up*. Here are two rules of thumb about beginning a sentence:

1. **Get to the subject of the main clause quickly.** Avoid beginning more than a few sentences with long introductory phrases and clauses.
2. **Get to the verb and object quickly.** Avoid long, abstract subjects and interruptions between subjects and verbs, and verbs and their objects.

Rule of Thumb 1: Get to the Subject Quickly We have a problem with sentences that open with long introductory phrases and clauses, because as we read them, we have to hold in mind that the subject and verb of a main clause are still to come, and that hinders easy understanding.

Compare these next examples. In (1b), we have to read and understand seventeen words while holding in mind that we have yet to reach the main subject and verb. In (1c), we get past the subject and verb of the first clause in just three words:

> 1b. **Since most undergraduate students change their major fields of study at least once during their college careers,** *first-year students* who are not certain about the program of studies they want to pursue SHOULD NOT LOAD UP their schedules to meet requirements for a particular program.

> ✓ 1c. **First-year students** SHOULD NOT LOAD UP their schedules with requirements for a particular program if they are not certain about the program of studies they want to pursue, because most CHANGE their major fields at least once during their college careers.

When you draft a sentence with a very long introductory clause, try moving it to the end. If it doesn't fit there, try turning it into a sentence of its own.

It is, however, a fact of English style that clauses beginning with *if, since, when*, and *although* tend to appear before main clauses rather than after. So if you cannot avoid opening with a subordinate clause, keep it short.

An exception: In a style called "periodic" or "suspended," writers deliberately pile up introductory subordinate clauses to delay and thereby heighten the impact of a concluding main clause:

> When a society spends more on its pets than it does on its homeless,
>
> when it rewards those who hit a ball the farthest more highly than those who care most deeply for its neediest,
>
> when it takes more interest in the juvenile behavior of its richest children than in the deficient education of its poorest,
>
> it has lost its moral center.

Used sparingly, this kind of sentence can have a dramatic impact, especially when the last few words of the last clause are appropriately stressed. We discuss this matter again in Lesson 9.

Rule of Thumb 2: Get Past the Verb and Object Quickly
Readers also want to get past the main subject to its verb and
object. Therefore,

- Keep subjects short.
- Avoid interrupting the subject-verb connection.
- Avoid interrupting the verb-object connection.

   Revise Long Subjects into Short Ones   Start by underlin-
ing whole subjects. If you find a long subject (more than seven
or eight words) including nominalizations, try turning the nominalization into a verb and finding a subject for it:

> **Abco Inc.'s *understanding* of the drivers of its profitability in
> the Asian market for small electronics** helped it pursue oppor-
> tunities in Africa.

> ✓ **Abco Inc.** was able to pursue opportunities in Africa because it
> understood what drove profitability in the Asian market for small
> electronics.

   A subject can also be long if it includes a long relative clause:

> A company **that focuses on hiring the best personnel and then
> trains them not just for the work they are hired to do but for
> higher-level jobs** is likely to earn the loyalty of its employees.

Try turning the relative clause into an introductory subordinate
clause beginning with *when* or *if:*

> **When a company focuses on hiring the best personnel and then
> trains them not just for the work they are hired to do but for
> higher-level jobs,** it is likely to earn the loyalty of its employees.

But if the introductory clause turns out to be as long as that
one, try moving it to the end of its sentence, especially if (1) the
main clause is short and to the point and (2) the moveable
clause expresses newer and more complex information that
supports or elaborates on the preceding main clause.

✓ A company is likely to earn the loyalty of its employees **when it focuses on hiring the best personnel and then trains them not just for the work they are hired to do but for higher-level jobs.**

Or better yet, perhaps, turn it into a sentence of its own.

✓ Some companies focus on hiring the best personnel and then train them not just for the work they are hired to do but for higher-level jobs later. **Such companies are likely to earn the loyalty of their employees.**

Avoid Interrupting the Subject-Verb Connection   You also frustrate readers when you interrupt the connection between a subject and verb, like this:

Some scientists, **because they write in a style that is impersonal and objective,** do not easily communicate with laypeople.

That *because* clause after the subject forces us to hold our mental breath until we reach the verb, *do not easily communicate.* Move the interruption to the beginning or end of its sentence, depending on whether it connects more closely to what precedes or follows it (note the *since* instead of *because*):

✓ Since some scientists write in a style that is impersonal and objective, they do **not easily communicate with laypeople. This lack of communication** damages . . .

✓ Some scientists do not easily communicate with laypeople because they write in **a style that is impersonal and objective. It is a kind of style** filled with passives and . . .

We mind short interruptions less:

✓ Some scientists **deliberately** write in a style that is impersonal and objective.

Avoid Interrupting the Verb-Object Connection   We also like to get past the verb to its object quickly. This sentence doesn't let us do that:

We must develop, **if we are to become competitive with other companies in our region,** a core of knowledge regarding the state of the art in effective industrial organizations.

Move the interrupting element to the beginning or end of its sentence, depending on what comes next:

✓ **If we are to compete with other companies in our region,** we must develop a core of knowledge about the state of the art in **effective industrial organizations. Such organizations provide . . .**

✓ **We** must develop a core of knowledge about the state of the art in effective industrial organizations **if we are to compete with other companies in our region. Increasing competition . . .**

An exception: When a prepositional phrase you can move is shorter than a long object, try putting the phrase between the verb and object:

In a long sentence, put the newest and most important information that you want your reader to remember **at its end.**

✓ In a long sentence, put **at its end** the newest and most important information that you want your reader to remember.

Here's the point: Readers read most easily when you quickly get them to the subject of your main clause and then past that subject to its verb and object. Avoid long introductory phrases and clauses, long subjects, and interruptions between subjects and verbs, and between verbs and objects.

Another Principle: Starting with Your Point

We've looked at four principles of style that help you start a sentence clearly and directly:

* Begin with its subject.
* Make that subject short, concrete, and already known to readers.

- Put a verb directly after it.
- Make that verb communicate a specific action.

We can add another principle, one that applies to long sentences in particular. Compare these two:

> High-deductible health plans and Health Saving Accounts into which workers and their employers make tax-deductible deposits result in workers' taking more responsibility for their health care.

> ✓ Workers take more responsibility for their health care when they adopt high-deductible insurance plans and Health Saving Accounts into which they and their employers deposit tax-deductible contributions.

Unlike that lumbering first sentence, the second follows those four principles: it begins not with a long, abstract subject but with a short, concrete one familiar to readers, directly followed by a verb stating a specific action: *Workers take. . . .*

But it differs in another way. In that first sentence, we have to read more than twenty words before we see their relevance to its key claim, to its *main point* about workers' taking responsibility for their health care. We have to read to its end to see the relevance of its beginning:

> [High-deductible health plans and Health Saving Accounts into which workers and their employers make tax-deductible deposits]$_{explanation/support}$ [result in workers' taking more responsibility for their health care.]$_{point}$

In contrast, the second sentence opens with an eight-word main clause stating its point clearly and concisely:

> ✓ [Workers take more responsibility for their health care]$_{point}$ [when they adopt high-deductible insurance plans and Health Saving Accounts into which they and their employers make tax-deductible deposits.]$_{explanation/support}$

When we read its point first, we can anticipate the relevance of the next nineteen words *even before we read them*.

Here is a very general principle about how we read: we can best manage complexity when we begin with something short and direct that frames the more complex information that follows. We have seen how that principle applies to individual subjects and verbs. But it also applies to the *logical* elements of a long sentence, to its point and to its explanation or supporting information. When a point is dribbled out or delayed, we have to reconstruct it, then mentally reassemble the sentence into its logical parts. A point clearly stated up front gives us a context to understand the complexity that follows.

To diagnose a long sentence, look first for its point, the key claim that you want readers to grasp quickly. If you find it in the middle of its sentence or at its end, revise: state it in a short, simple main clause at the beginning. Then add to it the longer, more complex information that supports or explains it. (See pp. 94, however, for a competing principle.)

In fact, this principle of simple-before-complex applies to even larger units:

- Begin a paragraph with a sentence (or two) expressing its point so that readers can understand what follows (see pp. 75–78 for more on this).

- Begin a section of a document with a paragraph or two stating its point.

- Do the same for a whole document: begin with an introduction that states its point and frames the rest.

Sentence, paragraph, section, or whole—how quickly, concisely, and *helpfully* you begin determines how easily your readers understand what follows.

Reshaping Sprawl

When we see the point of a sentence first, we can slog through whatever sprawling mess might follow. But we will wish we didn't have to. This next sentence begins with a clearly stated point, but then sprawls through a string of four explanatory subordinate clauses:

> No scientific advance is more exciting than genetic engineering,_{point} which is a new way of manipulating the elemental structural units of life itself, which are the genes and chromosomes that tell our cells how to reproduce to become the parts that constitute our bodies_{explanation}.

Graphically, it looks like this:

> No scientific advance is more exciting than genetic engineering, *[point and subject-verb core]*
>
>> **which** is a new way of manipulating the elemental structural units of life itself, *[tacked-on relative clause]*
>>
>>> **which** are the genes and chromosomes *[tacked-on relative clause]*
>>>
>>>> **that** tell our cells how to reproduce to become the parts *[tacked-on relative clause]*
>>>>
>>>>> **that** constitute our bodies. *[final tacked-on relative clause]*

Diagnose this problem by having someone read your prose aloud. If your reader hesitates, stumbles over words, or runs out of breath before getting to the end of a sentence, so will your silent reader. You can revise in four ways:

1. Cut

Try reducing some of the relative clauses to phrases by deleting *who/that/which* + *is/was*, etc.:

✓ Of the many areas of science important to our future, few are more promising than genetic engineering, ~~which is~~ a new way of manipulating the elemental structural units of life itself, ~~which are~~ the genes and chromosomes that tell our cells how to reproduce to become the parts that constitute our bodies.

Occasionally, you have to rewrite the remaining verb into an -*ing* form:

> The day is coming when we will all have numbers **that will identify** our financial transactions so that the IRS can monitor all activities **that involve** economic activity.
>
> ✓ The day is coming when we will all have numbers ~~that will~~ **identifying** our financial transactions so that the IRS can monitor all activities ~~that~~ **involving** economic activity.

2. Turn Subordinate Clauses into Independent Sentences

> ✓ Many areas of science are important to our future, but few are more promising than genetic engineering. **It is a new way of manipulating the elemental structural units of life itself, the genes and chromosomes that tell our cells how to reproduce to become the parts that constitute our bodies.**

If none of that works, you have to do some major restructuring.

3. Change Clauses to Modifying Phrases

You can write a long sentence but still avoid sprawl if you change relative clauses to one of three kinds of modifying phrases: resumptive, summative, or free. You have probably never heard of these terms before, but they name stylistic devices you have read many times and so should know how to use.

Resumptive Modifiers These two examples contrast a relative clause and a resumptive modifier:

> Since mature writers often use resumptive modifiers to extend a line of thought, we need a word to name what I have not done in this sentence, **which I could have ended after the word *sentence* but extended to show you a relative clause attached to a noun.**

✓ Since mature writers often use resumptive modifiers to extend a line of thought, we need a word to name what I am about to do in this sentence, **a sentence that I could have ended at that comma, but extended to show you how resumptive modifiers work.**

The boldface resumptive modifier repeats a key word, *sentence*, and rolls on.

To create a resumptive modifier, find a key noun just before the tacked on clause, then pause after it with a comma:

Since mature writers often use resumptive modifiers to extend a line of thought, we need a word to name what I am about to do in this **sentence,**

Then repeat the noun:

Since mature writers often use resumptive modifiers to extend a line of thought, we need a word to name what I am about to do in this **sentence,**

a sentence . . .

Then to that repeated word add a restrictive relative clause beginning with *that:*

Since mature writers often use resumptive modifiers to extend a line of thought, we need a word to name what I am about to do in this sentence,

a sentence **that I could have ended at that comma, but extended to show you how resumptive modifiers work.**

You can also resume with an adjective or verb. In that case, you don't add a relative clause; you just repeat the adjective or verb and continue.

✓ It was American writers who found a voice that was both **true** and **lyrical,**

true to the rhythms of the working man's speech and **lyrical** in its celebration of his labor.

✓ All who value independence should **resist** the trivialization of government regulation,

resist its obsession with administrative tidiness and compulsion to arrange things not for our convenience but for theirs.

Occasionally, you can create a resumptive modifier with the phrase *one that*. This sentence sprawls:

> I want now to address a problem we have wholly ignored that has plagued societies that sell their natural resources to benefit a few today rather than using them to develop new resources that benefit everyone tomorrow.

We can replace the first *that* with *one that*:

> ✓ I now address a problem we have wholly ignored, **one that** has plagued societies that sell their natural resources to benefit a few today rather than using them to develop new resources that benefit everyone tomorrow.

Summative Modifiers   Here are two sentences that contrast relative clauses and summative modifiers. Notice how the *which* in the first one feels "tacked on":

> Economic changes have reduced Russian population growth to less than zero, **which will have serious social implications.**
> ✓ Economic changes have reduced Russian population growth to less than zero, **a demographic event that will have serious social implications.**

To create a summative modifier, end a grammatically complete segment of a sentence with a comma:

> Economic changes have reduced Russian population growth to less than zero,

Find a term that sums up the substance of the sentence so far:

> Economic changes have reduced Russian population growth to less than zero,
>
> **a demographic event . . .**

Then continue with a restrictive relative clause beginning with *that:*

> Economic changes have reduced Russian population growth to less than zero,
>> a demographic event **that will have serious social implications.**

A summative modifier has the same effect as a resumptive modifier: it lets you bring a clause to a sense of closure, then begin afresh.

Free Modifiers   Like the other modifiers, a free modifier can appear at the end of a clause, but instead of repeating a key word or summing up what went before, it comments on the subject of the closest verb:

> ✓ Free modifiers resemble resumptive and summative modifiers, **letting you** [i.e., the free modifier lets you] **extend the line of a sentence while avoiding a train of ungainly phrases and clauses.**

Free modifiers usually begin with an -*ing* present participle, as that one did, but they can also begin with a past participle verb, like this:

> ✓ Leonardo da Vinci was a man of powerful intellect,
>> *driven* **by** [i.e., Leonardo was driven by] **an insatiable curiosity**
>> and
>> *haunted* **by a vision of artistic perfection.**

A free modifier can also begin with an adjective:

> ✓ In 1939, we began to assist the British against Germany,
>> *aware* [i.e., we were aware] **that we faced another world war.**

We call these modifiers *free* because they can both begin and end a sentence:

> ✓ **Driven by an insatiable curiosity,** Leonardo da Vinci was . . .
> ✓ **Aware that we faced another world war,** in 1939 we began . . .

Here's the point: When you have to write a long sentence, don't just add one phrase or clause after another, willy-nilly. Particularly avoid tacking one relative clause onto another onto another. Try extending the line of a sentence with resumptive, summative, and free modifiers.

---

4. Coordinate

Coordination is the real foundation of a gracefully shaped sentence. It's harder to create good coordination than good modifiers, but when done well, it's more pleasing to the reader. Compare these. My version is first; the original is second:

> The aspiring artist may find that even a minor, unfinished work which was botched may be an instructive model for how things should be done, while for the amateur spectator, such works are the daily fare which may provide good, honest nourishment, which can lead to an appreciation of deeper pleasures that are also more refined.

> ✓ For the aspiring artist, the minor, the unfinished, or even the botched work, may be an instructive model for how things should—and should not—be done. For the amateur spectator, such works are the daily fare which provide good, honest nourishment—and which can lead to appreciation of more refined, or deeper pleasures.

> —Eva Hoffman, "Minor Art Offers Special Pleasures"

My revision sprawls through a string of tacked-on clauses:

> The aspiring artist may find that even a minor, unfinished work
>   **which** was botched may be an instructive model for
>   **how** things should be done,
>   **while** for the amateur spectator, such works are the daily fare
>   **which** may provide good, honest nourishment,
>   **which** can lead to an appreciation of deeper pleasures
>   **that** are also more refined.

Hoffman's original gets its shape from its multiple coordinations. Structurally, it looks like this:

For the aspiring artist,
{
the minor,
the unfinished,
or
even the botched
}
work may be

an instructive model for how things
{
should
and
should not
}
be done.

For the amateur spectator, such works are

the daily fare
{
which provide
{
good,
honest
}
nourishment—

and

which can lead to appreciation of
{
more refined,
or
deeper
}
pleasures.
}

That second sentence in particular shows how elaborate coordination can get.

A General Design Principle: Short to Long   We should note a feature that distinguishes well-formed coordination. You can hear it if you read this next sentence aloud:

> We should devote a few final words to a matter that reaches beyond the techniques of research to the connections between those subjective values that reflect our deepest ethical choices and objective research.

That sentence seems to end too abruptly with *objective research.* Structurally, it looks like this:

$$
\ldots \text{ between }
\left\{
\begin{array}{c}
\text{those subjective values that reflect our} \\
\text{deepest ethical choices} \\
\text{and} \\
\text{objective research.}
\end{array}
\right\}
$$

This next revision moves from shorter to longer by reversing the two coordinate elements and by adding a parallelism to the second one to make it longer still. Read this one aloud:

✓ We should devote a few final words to a matter that reaches beyond the techniques of research to the connections between objective research and those subjective values that reflect our deepest ethical choices and strongest intellectual commitments.

Structurally, it looks like this:

$$
✔ \ldots \text{ between }
\left\{
\begin{array}{c}
\text{objective research} \\
\text{and} \\
\text{those subjective} \\
\text{values that reflect our}
\end{array}
\left\{
\begin{array}{c}
\text{deepest ethical choices} \\
\text{and} \\
\text{strongest intellectual} \\
\text{commitments.}
\end{array}
\right.
\right\}
$$

A characteristics of especially elegant prose is how its writers elaborate all these devices for extending the line of a sentence, especially balanced coordination. I will discuss those devices and their elaboration in Lesson 9.

> ***Here's the point:***   Coordination lets you extend the line of a sentence more gracefully than just by tacking on one element to another. When you can coordinate, try to order the elements so that they go from shorter to longer, from simpler to more complex.

A Unifying Principle   This principle of short-to-long is, in fact, one of the unifying principles of a clear prose style:

- It applies to the subject-verb sequence of individual sentences: the shorter the better to introduce the longer, more complex elements that follow.

- It applies to the principle of old-new: old information is usually objectively shorter than new information, but it is "psychologically" shorter, as well.

- It applies to ordering the logical elements of a long sentence: begin with its short point, then add the longer and more complex information that explains or supports it.

- It applies again here in balanced coordination: put shorter elements before longer ones.

TROUBLESHOOTING LONG SENTENCES

Even when you manage their internal structures, though, long sentences can still go wrong.

Faulty Grammatical Coordination

Ordinarily, we coordinate elements only of the same grammatical structure: clause and clause, prepositional phrase and prepositional phrase, and so on. When you coordinate different grammatical structures, readers may feel you have created an offensive lack of parallelism. Careful writers avoid this:

The committee recommends { **revising the curriculum** to recognize trends in local employment
and
that the division be reorganized to reflect the new curriculum. }

They would correct that to this:

✔ . . . recommends
$$\left\{ \begin{array}{l} \textbf{that the curriculum be revised} \\ \text{to recognize} \ldots \\ \qquad\qquad \text{and} \\ \textbf{that the division be reorganized} \\ \text{to reflect.} \ldots \end{array} \right\}$$

Or to this:

✔ . . . recommends
$$\left\{ \begin{array}{l} \textbf{revising the curriculum} \\ \text{to recognize} \ldots \\ \qquad\qquad \text{and} \\ \textbf{reorganizing the division} \\ \text{to reflect.} \ldots \end{array} \right\}$$

However, some nonparallel coordinations do occur in well-written prose. Careful writers coordinate a noun phrase with a *how* clause:

✔ We will attempt to delineate
$$\left\{ \begin{array}{l} \textbf{the problems} \text{ of education} \\ \text{in developing nations} \\ \qquad\qquad \text{and} \\ \textbf{how coordinated efforts} \\ \textbf{can address} \text{ them in} \\ \text{economical ways.} \end{array} \right\}$$

They coordinate an adverb with a prepositional phrase:

✔ The proposal appears to have been written
$$\left\{ \begin{array}{l} \textbf{quickly,} \\ \textbf{carefully,} \\ \qquad \text{and} \\ \textbf{with the help} \text{ of many.} \end{array} \right\}$$

Careful readers do not blink at either.

Faulty Rhetorical Coordination

We respond to coordination best when the elements are coordinate not only in grammar but in thought. Some inexperienced writers coordinate by just joining one element to another with *and:*

> Grade inflation is a problem at many universities, ***and*** it leads to a devaluation of good grades earned by hard work ***and*** will not be solved simply by grading harder.

Those *and*s obscure the relationships among those claims:

> ✓ Grade inflation is a problem at many universities, **because** it devalues good grades that were earned by hard work, **but** it will not be solved simply by grading harder.

Unfortunately, I can't tell you how to recognize when elements are not coordinate in thought, except to say, "Watch for it." Which, of course, is like someone telling us to "hit the ball squarely." We know that. What we don't know is how.

Unclear Connections

Readers are also bothered by a coordination so long that they lose track of its internal connections and pronoun references:

> Teachers should remember that students are vulnerable and uncertain about those everyday ego-bruising moments that adults ignore and that they do not understand that one day they will become as confident and as secure as the adults that bruise them.

We sense a flicker of hesitation about where to connect:

> . . . and that they do not understand that one day they . . .

To revise a sentence like that, shorten the first half of the coordination so that you can start the second half closer to the point where the coordination began:

> ✓ Teachers should remember that students are vulnerable to ego-bruising moments that adults ignore and that they do not understand that one day . . .

If you can't do that, repeat a word that reminds the reader where the coordination began (thereby creating a resumptive modifier):

✓ Teachers should try to remember that students are vulnerable to ego-bruising moments that adults ignore, **to remember** that they do not understand that . . .

Ambiguous Modifiers

Another problem with modifiers is that sometimes readers are unsure what they modify:

Overtaxing oneself in physical activity too frequently results in injury.

What happens too frequently, overtaxing or injuries? We can make its meaning unambiguous by moving *too frequently:*

✓ Overtaxing oneself too frequently in physical activity results in injury.
✓ Overtaxing oneself in physical activity results too frequently in injury.

A modifier at the end of a clause can ambiguously modify either a neighboring or a more distant phrase:

Scientists have learned that their observations are as subjective as those in any other field **in recent years.**

We can move the modifier to a less ambiguous position:

✓ **In recent years,** scientists have learned that . . .
✓ Scientists have learned that **in recent years** their . . .

Here's the point: Even well-constructed long sentences can give readers a problem if they can't connect the second part of a coordination to its starting point or if they are unsure about what a phrase actually modifies.

Dangling Modifiers

Another problem with a long sentence can be a dangling modifier. A modifier dangles when its implied subject differs from
the explicit subject of the main clause:

> To overcome chronic poverty and lagging economic development
> in sub-Saharan Africa,_{dangling modifier} a commitment to health and
> education_{whole subject} is necessary for there to be progress in raising
> standards of living.

The implied subject of *address* is some unnamed agent, but the
explicit subject of the main clause is *commitment*. To undangle
the modifier, we make its implicit subject explicit:

> ✓ If **developed countries** are to overcome chronic poverty and lag-
> ging economic development in sub-Saharan Africa, a commitment
> to health and education is necessary . . .

Or better, make the implicit subject of the modifier the explicit
subject of the clause:

> ✓ To overcome chronic poverty and lagging economic development
> in sub-Saharan Africa, **developed countries** must commit them-
> selves to . . .

INTRINSIC SENSE

You can use these devices to shape a long yet clear sentence,
but not even the best syntax can salvage incoherent content.
This next sentence appeared in a Sunday *New York Times* travel
section. The sentence before it had introduced the professional
women of Amsterdam's red-light district:

> They are so unself-conscious about their profession that by day
> they can be seen standing naked in doorways, chatting with their
> neighbors in the shadow of the Oudekerstoren Church, which of-
> fers Saturday carillon concerts at 4 P.M. and a panoramic view of
> the city from its tower in summer.

This syntactically well-formed sentence opens with a coherent
clause:

They are so unself-conscious about their profession that by day they can be seen standing naked in doorways . . .

It continues with a free modifier:

. . . chatting with their neighbors in the shadow of the Oudekerstoren Church . . .

then concludes with a relative clause with a balanced pair of direct objects:

. . . which offers $\left\{ \begin{array}{c} \text{Saturday carillon concerts at 4 P.M.} \\ \text{and} \\ \text{a panoramic view of the city from} \\ \text{its tower in summer.} \end{array} \right\}$

But the movement of ideas is goofy (or evidence of a sly sense of humor). It fails a principle put forward by the 19th century philosopher John Stuart Mill:

The structure of every sentence is a lesson in logic.

9

Elegance

Anything is better than not to write clearly. There is nothing to be said against lucidity, and against simplicity only the possibility of dryness. This is a risk well worth taking when you reflect how much better it is to be bald than to wear a curly wig.
—SOMERSET MAUGHAM

UNDERSTANDING ELEGANCE

Anyone who can write clearly, concisely, and coherently should rejoice to have achieved so much. But while most of us prefer bald clarity to the density of institutional prose, others feel that relentless simplicity can be dry, even arid. It has the spartan virtue of unsalted meat and potatoes, but such fare is rarely memorable. A flash of elegance can not only fix a thought in our minds, but give us a flicker of pleasure every time we recall it. Unfortunately, I can't tell you how to do that. In fact, I incline toward those who think that the most elegant elegance is disarming simplicity.

Nevertheless, there are a few devices that can shape a thought in ways that are both elegant and clear. Just knowing them, however, is about as useful as just knowing the ingredients in the bouillabaisse of a great cook, then thinking you can make it. Knowing ingredients and knowing how to use them distinguish reading cookbooks and Cooking. Maybe elegant clarity is a gift. But even a gift has to be educated and exercised.

Balance and Symmetry

What most makes a sentence graceful is a balance and symmetry among its parts, one echoing another in sound, rhythm, structure, and meaning. A skilled writer can balance almost any parts of a sentence, but the most common balance is based on coordination.

Balanced Coordination   Here is a balanced passage and my revision of it. A tin ear can distinguish which is which:

> The national unity of a free people depends upon a sufficiently even balance of political power to make it impracticable for the administration to be arbitrary and for the opposition to be revolutionary and irreconcilable. Where that balance no longer exists, democracy perishes. For unless all the citizens of a state are forced by circumstances to compromise, unless they feel that they can affect policy but that no one can wholly dominate it, unless by habit and necessity they have to give and take, freedom cannot be maintained.
>
> —Walter Lippmann

> The national unity of a free people depends upon a sufficiently even balance of political power to make it impracticable for an administration to be arbitrary against a revolutionary opposition that is irreconcilably opposed to it. Where that balance no longer exists, democracy perishes, because unless all the citizens of a state are habitually forced by necessary circumstances to compromise in a way that lets them affect policy with no one dominating it, freedom cannot be maintained.

My sentences lurch from one part to the next. In Lippmann's, we hear one clause and phrase echo another in word order, sound, and meaning, giving the whole passage an intricate architectural symmetry.

If we extend the idea of topic and stress from a whole sentence to its parts, we can see how he balances even short segments. Note how each significant word in one phrase echoes another in its corresponding one (I boldface topics of phrases and italicize stresses):

The national unity of a free people depends upon a sufficiently even balance of political power to make it impracticable

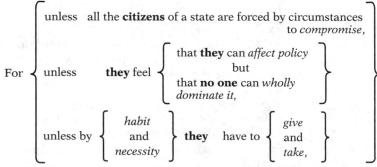

for **the administration** to be *arbitrary*

and

for **the opposition** to be

revolutionary
and
irreconcilable.

Lippmann balances the phrasal topics of *administration* and *opposition,* and closes by balancing the stressed sounds and meanings of *arbitrary, revolutionary,* and *irreconcilable.* He follows with a short concluding sentence whose stressed words are not coordinated, but still balanced (I use square brackets to indicate noncoordinated balance):

Where [**that balance** *no longer exists,*
           democracy   *perishes.*]

Then he creates an especially intricate design, balancing many sounds and meanings:

For

unless   all the **citizens** of a state are forced by circumstances
                                                 to *compromise,*

unless   **they** feel

that **they** can *affect policy*
but
that **no one** can *wholly dominate it,*

unless by

habit
and
necessity

they   have to

give
and
take,

freedom cannot be *maintained.*

- He repeats *citizens* as the subject/topic of each clause: *all the citizens, they, they* (note the passive in the first one: *citizens **are forced;** the active version would have unbalanced the coordination).

- He balances the sound and sense of *force* against *feel,* and the meaning of *affect policy* against the meaning of *dominate it.*

- In the last *unless* clause, he balances the meaning of *habit* against *necessity,* and the stressed *give* against *take.*

- He balances the meanings of *compromise, affect, dominate,* and *give and take.*

- Then to balance the clauses of that short preceding sentence, *balance no longer exists—democracy perishes,* he concludes with an equally short clause, *freedom cannot be maintained,* whose meaning and structure echo the corresponding pair in the preceding sentence:

balance	no longer exists
democracy	perishes
freedom	cannot be maintained

For those who notice and care, it is an impressive construction.

Uncoordinated Balance   We can also balance structures that are not grammatically coordinate. In this example, the subject balances the object.

Scientists whose research	*creates revolutionary views of the universe*
invariably upset	
those of us who	*construct our vision of reality out of our common-sense experience of it.*

Here, the predicate (everything after the subject) of a relative clause in a subject balances the predicate of the sentence:

A government ⎡ that is unwilling to *listen* to the *moderate hopes* of *its citizenry*

must eventually *answer* to the *harsh justice* of *its revolutionaries.* ⎤

Here a direct object balances the object of a preposition:

Those of us concerned with our school systems will not sacrifice

⎡ the *intellectual growth* of   our *innocent children*
                          to
the *social engineering* of   *incompetent bureaucrats.* ⎤

A more complicated balance:

Were I trading[1a] ⎡ scholarly principles[2a]
for
financial security,[2b] ⎤

I would not be writing[1b] ⎡ short books[3a]
on
minor subjects[3b]
for
small audiences.[3c] ⎤

In that sentence,

- A subordinate clause (**1A**), *Were I trading,* balances the main clause (**1B**), *I would not be writing.*

- The object of that subordinate clause (**2A**), *scholarly principles*, balances the object in the prepositional phrase (**2B**), *financial security.*

- The object in the main clause (**3A**), *short books,* balances objects in two prepositional phrases, (**1B**), *minor subjects,* and (**3C**), *small audiences* (with the balanced *short, minor,* and *small*).

Remember that you usually create the most rhythmical balance when each succeeding balanced element is a bit longer than the previous one.

These patterns even encourage you to think in ways that you might not have otherwise. In that sense, they don't just shape your thinking; they generate it. Suppose you begin a sentence like this:

> In his earliest years, Picasso was a master draftsman of the traditional human form.

Now try this:

> In his earliest years, Picasso was **not only** a master draftsman of the traditional human form, **but also** . . .

Now you have to wonder what else he might have been. Or not have been.

I should cite another device that often appears in elegant prose, one described in Lesson 8—resumptive and summative modifiers:

> The British Empire brought its version of administrative bureaucratic order to societies around the globe, **an order that would endure in those lands long after Britons retreated to their own shores.**

> When the poem *Howl* first appeared, the "Beats" and other avant-gardes celebrated it as a revolutionary critique of the postwar American world, **a view not shared by most mainstream literary critics, who considered it incoherent rant.**

> ***Here's the point:***   The most striking feature of elegant prose is balanced sentence structures. You most easily balance one part of a sentence against another by coordinating them with *and, or, nor, but,* and *yet,* but you can also balance noncoordinated phrases and clauses. Used to excess, these patterns can seem merely clever, but used prudently, they can emphasize an important point or conclude a line of reasoning with a flourish that careful readers notice.

CLIMACTIC EMPHASIS

How you begin a sentence determines its clarity; how you end it determines its rhythm and grace. We've already seen one device: balanced coordination. There are five others.

1. Weighty Words

When we get close to the end of a sentence, we expect words that deserve stress, so we may feel a sentence is anticlimactic if it ends on words of slight grammatical or semantic weight. At the end of a sentence, prepositions feel light—a reason we sometimes avoid leaving one there. The rhythm of a sentence should carry readers toward strength. Compare:

> Studies into intellectual differences among races is a project that only the most politically naive psychologist is willing to give support to.

> ✓ Studies into intellectual differences among races is a project that only the most politically naive scientist is willing to support.

Adjectives and adverbs are heavier than prepositions, but lighter than verbs or nouns, the heaviest of which are nominalizations. Readers have problems with nominalizations in the subject of a sentence, but at the end they provide a satisfyingly climactic thump, particularly when two of them are in coordinate balance. Consider this excerpt from Winston Churchill's "Finest Hour" speech. Churchill ended it with a parallelism climaxed by a balanced pair of nouns:

> . . . until in God's good time,

the New World, with all its $\left\{ \begin{array}{c} \text{power} \\ \text{and} \\ \text{might} \end{array} \right\}$ steps forth to

$\left\{ \begin{array}{c} \text{the } \textbf{rescue} \\ \text{and} \\ \text{the } \textbf{liberation} \end{array} \right\}$ of the old.

He could have written more simply, and more banally:

> . . . until the New World rescues us.

2. *Of* + Weighty Word

This seems unlikely, but it's true. Look at how Churchill ends his sentence: The light *of* (followed by a lighter *a* or *the*) quickens the rhythm of a sentence just before the stress of the climactic monosyllable, *old:*

> . . . the rescue and the liberation of the **old.**

We associate this pattern with self-conscious elegance, as in the first few sentences of Edward Gibbon's *History of the Decline and Fall of the Roman Empire* (contrast that title with *History of the Roman Empire's Decline and Fall*):

✓ In the second century of the Christian era, the Empire of Rome comprehended **the fairest part *of* the earth,** AND **the most civilized portion *of* mankind.** The frontiers of that extensive monarchy were guarded **by ancient renown** AND **disciplined valour.**

The gentle but powerful influence of laws and manners had gradually cemented **the union** *of* **the provinces.** Their peaceful inhabitants **enjoyed AND abused the advantages** *of* **wealth AND luxury.** The image of a free constitution was preserved with decent **reverence:** the Roman senate appeared to possess the sovereign authority, and devolved on the emperors all **the executive powers** *of* **government.**

In comparison, this is flat:

In the second century AD, the Roman Empire comprehended **the earth's fairest, most civilized part.** Ancient renown and disciplined valour guarded **its extensive frontiers.** The gentle but powerful influence of laws and manners had gradually **unified the provinces.** Their peaceful inhabitants enjoyed and abused luxurious wealth while decently preserving what seemed to be **a free constitution.** Appearing to possess the sovereign authority, the Roman senate devolved on the emperors all **executive governmental powers.**

3. Echoing Salience

At the end of a sentence, readers hear special emphasis when a stressed word or phrase balances the sound or meaning of an earlier one. (These examples are all from Peter Gay's *Style in History.*)

✓ I have written these essays to anatomize this familiar yet really strange being, **style the centaur;** the book may be read as an extended critical commentary on Buffon's famous saying that **the style is the man.**

When we hear a stressed word echo an earlier one, these balances become even more emphatic:

✓ Apart from a few mechanical tricks of rhetoric, **manner** is indissolubly linked to **matter; style shapes,** and in turn is **shaped** by, **substance.**

✓ It seems frivolous, almost inappropriate, to be **stylish** about **style.**

Gay echoes both the sound and meaning of *manner* in *matter, style* in *substance, shapes* in *shaped by,* and *stylish* in *style.*

4. Chiasmus

This device (pronounced kye-AZZ-muss) is interesting perhaps only to those fascinated with the most arcane figures of style. The word *chiasmus* is from the Greek word for 'crossing.' It balances elements in two parts of a sentence, but the second part reverses the order of the elements in the first part. For example, this next sentence would be both coordinate and parallel, but it does not end with a chiasmus, because the elements in the two parts are in the same order (1A1B : 2A2B):

✔ A concise style
can improve both

$\left\{ \begin{array}{c} \textbf{our own}^{1A} \; thinking^{1B} \\ \text{and} \\ \textbf{our readers'}^{2A} \; understanding.^{2B} \end{array} \right\}$

Were we seeking a special effect, we could reverse the order of elements in the second part to mirror those in the first. Now the pattern is not 1A1B : 2A2B, but rather 1A1B : 2B2A:

✔ A concise style
can improve not only

$\left\{ \begin{array}{c} \textbf{our own}^{1A} \; thinking^{1B} \\ \text{but} \\ \text{the } understanding^{2B} \textbf{ of our readers.}^{2A} \end{array} \right\}$

The next example is more complex. The first two elements are parallel, but the last three mirror one another: **AB CDE : AB EDC**:

$$\begin{bmatrix} \text{You}^{\textbf{A}} \quad \text{reveal}^{\textbf{B}} \quad \textbf{your own}^{\textbf{C}} \quad \textit{highest rhetorical}^{\textbf{D}} \quad \text{SKILL}^{\textbf{E}} \\ \qquad\qquad\quad \text{by the way} \\ \text{you}^{\textbf{A}} \quad \text{respect}^{\textbf{B}} \quad \text{THE BELIEFS}^{\textbf{E}} \quad \textit{most deeply held}^{\textbf{D}} \quad \textbf{by your reader.}^{\textbf{C}} \end{bmatrix}$$

5. Suspension

Finally, you can wind up a sentence with a dramatic climax by ignoring some earlier advice. In Lesson 8 I advised you to open your sentence with its point. But self-consciously elegant writers often open a sentence with a series of parallel and coordinated phrases and clauses just so that they can delay and thereby increase a sense of climax:

> If [journalists] held themselves as responsible for the rise of public cynicism as they hold "venal" politicians and the "selfish" public; if they considered that the license they have to criticize and defame comes with an implied responsibility to serve the public—if they did all or any of these things, they would make journalism more useful, public life, stronger, and themselves far more worthy of esteem.
>
> —James Fallows, *Breaking the News*

That sentence (the last one in Fallows's book) ends with a triple coordination. He ends it on its longest member, one that itself ends with an *of* + nominalization (*worthy of esteem*). Like all such devices, however, the impact of a long suspension is inversely proportional to its use; i.e., the less it's used, the bigger its bang.

Here's the point: An elegant sentence should end on strength. You can create that strength in five ways:

1. End with a strong word, or better, a pair of them.

2. End with a prepositional phrase introduced by *of*.

3. End with an echoing salience.

4. End with a chiasmus.

5. Delay the point of the sentence with a series of suspended clauses.

EXTRAVAGANT ELEGANCE

When writers combine all these elements in a single sentence, we know they are aiming at something special, as in this next passage:

> Far from being locked inside our own skins, inside the "dungeons" of ourselves, we are now able to recognize that our minds belong, quite naturally, to a collective "mind," a mind in which we share everything that is mental, most obviously language itself, and that the old boundary of the skin is not boundary at all but a membrane connecting the inner and outer experience of existence. Our intelligence, our wit, our cleverness, our unique personalities—all are simultaneously "our own" possessions and the world's.
>
> —Joyce Carol Oates, "New Heaven and New Earth"

Here is the anatomy of that passage:

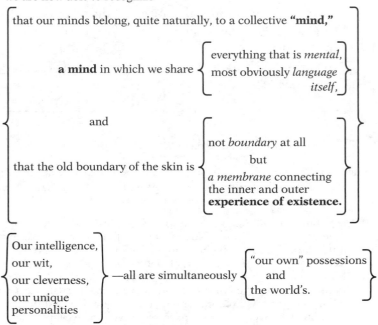

Far from being locked **inside** our own skins,

          inside the "dungeons" of ourselves,

we are now able to recognize

that our minds belong, quite naturally, to a collective **"mind,"**

a mind in which we share { everything that is *mental*, most obviously *language itself*, }

and

that the old boundary of the skin is { not *boundary* at all but *a membrane* connecting the inner and outer **experience of existence.** }

{ Our intelligence, our wit, our cleverness, our unique personalities } —all are simultaneously { "our own" possessions and the world's. }

In addition to all the coordination, note the two resumptive modifiers:

    Far from being locked **inside** our own skins,

            inside the "dungeons" of ourselves . . .

    our minds belong . . . to a collective **"mind,"**

            a mind in which we share . . .

Note as well the two nominalizations stressed at the end of the first sentence and the coordinate nominalizations at the end of the second:

> . . . the inner and outer experience of existence.

> . . . "our own" possessions and the world's.

But such patterns can be more elaborate yet. Here is the last sentence from Frederick Jackson Turner's *The Frontier in American History:*

> This then is the heritage of the pioneer experience—a passionate belief that a democracy was possible which should leave the individual a part to play in a free society and not make him a cog in a machine operated from above; which trusted in the common man, in his tolerance, his ability to adjust differences with good humor, and to work out an American type from the contributions of all nations—a type for which he would fight against those who challenged it in arms, and for which in time of war he would make sacrifices, even the temporary sacrifice of his individual freedom and his life, lest that freedom be lost forever.

Note the following:

- the summative modifier in the opening segment: *a passionate belief that . . .*

- the increased length and weight of the second element in each coordination, even the coordinations inside coordinations

- the two resumptive modifiers beginning with *type* and *sacrifice*

That may be over the top, especially the quadruple chiasmus in the last sixteen words:

the temporary[1] <u>sacrifice</u>[2]   of his individual FREEDOM[3] and *his life,*[4]
lest[4]   that FREEDOM[3] be   <u>lost</u>[2]   **forever.**[1]

The meaning of *temporary* balances *forever; sacrifice* balances *lost; freedom* echoes *freedom;* and the sound of *life* balances *lest* (not to mention the near rhyme of *lest* in *lost*). You just don't see that kind of sentence anymore.

Here is the anatomy of that sentence:

This then is the heritage of the pioneer experience—
[summative modifier]   a passionate belief that a democracy was possible

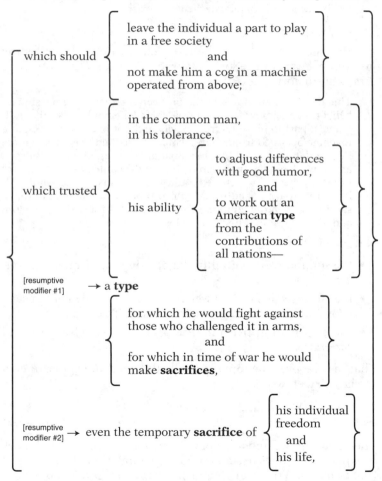

which should {
leave the individual a part to play in a free society
and
not make him a cog in a machine operated from above;

which trusted {
in the common man,
in his tolerance,
his ability {
to adjust differences with good humor,
and
to work out an American **type** from the contributions of all nations—

[resumptive modifier #1] → a **type**

for which he would fight against those who challenged it in arms,
and
for which in time of war he would make **sacrifices**,

[resumptive modifier #2] → even the temporary **sacrifice** of {
his individual freedom
and
his life,

lest that freedom be lost forever.

NUANCES OF LENGTH AND RHYTHM

Most writers don't plan the length of their sentences, but that's not a problem, unless every sentence is shorter than fifteen or so words, or much longer. Artful writers, however, do use the length of a sentence for a purpose. Some write short sentences to strike a note of urgency:

> Toward noon Petrograd again became the field of military action; rifles and machine guns rang out everywhere. It was not easy to tell who was shooting or where. One thing was clear; the past and the future were exchanging shots. There was much casual firing; young boys were shooting off revolvers unexpectedly acquired. The arsenal was wrecked. . . . Shots rang out on both sides. But the board fence stood in the way, dividing the soldiers from the revolution. The attackers decided to break down the fence. They broke down part of it and set fire to the rest. About twenty barracks came into view. The bicyclists were concentrated in two or three of them. The empty barracks were set fire to at once.
>
> —Leon Trotsky, *The Russian Revolution*, trans. Max Eastman

Or terse certainty:

> The teacher or lecturer is a danger. He very seldom recognizes his nature or his position. The lecturer is a man who must talk for an hour. France may possibly have acquired the intellectual leadership of Europe when their academic period was cut down to 40 minutes. I also have lectured. The lecturer's first problem is to have enough words to fill 40 or 60 minutes. The professor is paid for his time, his results are almost impossible to estimate. . . . No teacher has ever failed from ignorance. That is empiric professional knowledge. Teachers fail because they cannot "handle the class." Real education must ultimately be limited to men who INSIST on knowing, the rest is mere sheep-herding.
>
> —Ezra Pound, *ABC of Reading*

Or passion. Here, D. H. Lawrence breaks what could have been a long paragraph and long sentences into fragmented outbursts.

Let us look at this American artist first. How did he ever get to America, to start with? Why isn't he a European still, like his father before him?

Now listen to me, don't listen to him. He'll tell you the lie you expect. Which is partly your fault for expecting it.

He didn't come in search of freedom of worship. England had more freedom of worship in the year 1700 than America had. Won by Englishmen who wanted freedom and so stopped at home and fought for it. And got it. Freedom of worship? Read the history of New England during the first century of its existence.

Freedom anyhow? The land of the free! This the land of the free! Why, if I say anything that displeases them, the free mob will lynch me, and that's my freedom. Free? Why I have never been in any country where the individual has such an abject fear of his fellow countrymen. Because, as I say, they are free to lynch him the moment he shows he is not one of them. . . .

All right then, what did they come for? For lots of reasons. Perhaps least of all in search of freedom of any sort: positive freedom, that is.

—D. H. Lawrence, *Studies in Classic American Literature*

Self-conscious stylists also write extravagantly long sentences. Here is just a piece of one whose sinuous length seems to mirror the confused progress of a protest march:

In any event, up at the front of this March, in the first line, back of that hollow square of monitors, Mailer and Lowell walked in this barrage of cameras, helicopters, TV cars, monitors, loudspeakers, and wavering buckling twisting line of notables, arms linked (line twisting so much that at times the movement was in file, one arm locked ahead, one behind, then the line would undulate about and the other arm would be ahead) speeding up a few steps, slowing down while a great happiness came back into the day as if finally one stood under some mythical arch in the great vault of history, helicopters buzzing about, chop-chop, and the sense of America divided on this day now liberated some undiscovered patriotism in Mailer so that he felt a sharp searing love for his country in this moment and on this day, crossing some divide in his own mind wider than the Potomac, a love so lacerated he felt as if a marriage were being torn and children lost—never does one love so much as then, obviously, then—and an odor of wood smoke, from where you knew not, was also in the air, a smoke of dignity and some calm heroism, not unlike the sense of freedom which also comes when a marriage is burst—Mailer knew for the first time why men in the front line of battle are almost always ready to die; there is a promise of some swift transit . . . [it goes on]

—Norman Mailer, *The Armies of the Night*

We almost feel we are eavesdropping on Mailer's stream of thought. But of course, such a sentence is the product not of an overflow of feeling but of premeditated art.

- Mailer opens with short, staccato phrases to suggest confusion, but he controls them by coordination.

- He continues the sentence by coordinating free modifiers: *arms linked . . .(line twisting . . .) speeding up . . .*

- After several more free modifiers, he continues with a resumptive modifier: *a love so lacerated . . .*

- After another grammatical sentence, he adds another resumptive modifier: *a smoke of dignity and some calm heroism . . .*

Here's the point: Think about the length of your sentences only if they are all longer than thirty words or so or shorter than fifteen. Your sentences will vary naturally if you edit them in the ways you've seen here. But if the occasion allows, don't be reluctant to experiment.

You won't acquire an elegant style just by reading this book. You must read those who write elegantly until their style runs along your muscles and nerves. Only then can you look at your own prose and know when it is elegant or just inflated. To that end, you might keep in mind George Bernard Shaw's advice to young writers:

In literature the ambition of the novice is to acquire the literary language; the struggle of the adept is to get rid of it.

The Ethics of Style

Ethics is in origin the art of recommending to others the
sacrifices required for cooperation with oneself.
—BERTRAND RUSSELL

BEYOND POLISH

It is easy to think that style is just the polish that makes a sentence go down smoothly, but more than easy reading is at stake in choosing subjects and verbs in these two sentences:

1a. **Shiites and Sunnis** DISTRUST one another because **they** HAVE ENGAGED in generations of cultural conflict.

1b. **Generations of cultural conflict** HAVE CREATED distrust between Shiites and Sunnis.

Which sentence more accurately reflects what causes the distrust between the two—their deliberate actions, as in (1a), or, as in (1b), the circumstances of their history? Such a choice of subjects and verbs even implies a philosophy of human action: do we freely choose to act, or do circumstances cause us to? Later, we'll look at the way this issue plays itself out in our own Declaration of Independence.

In fact, our choice of what character to tell a story about—people or their circumstances—involves more than ease of reading, even more than a philosophy of action, because every such choice also has an ethical dimension.

THE ETHICAL RESPONSIBILITIES OF WRITERS AND READERS

In the last nine lessons, I have emphasized the responsibility writers owe readers to write clearly. But readers also have a responsibility to read closely enough to understand ideas that require more than Dick-and-Jane sentences. It would be impossible, for example, for an engineer to revise this into language clear to everyone:

> The drag force on a particle of diameter d moving with speed u relative to a fluid of density p and viscosity μ is usually modeled by $F = 0.5C_D u^2 A$, where A is the cross-sectional area of the particle at right angles to the motion.

Most of us do work hard to understand—at least until we decide that a writer failed to work equally hard to help us understand or, worse, has deliberately made our reading more difficult than it has to be. Once we decide that a writer is careless, lazy, or willfully difficult—well, our days are too few to spend them on those indifferent to our needs.

But that response to gratuitous complexity only re-emphasizes how responsible we are to write clearly, for it seems axiomatic that if we don't want others to impose carelessly complex writing on us, then we ought not impose it on others. If we are socially responsible writers, we should make our ideas no simpler than they deserve, but no harder than they require.

Responsible writers follow a rule whose more general theme you probably recognize:

> Write to others as you would have others write to you.

Few of us violate that principle deliberately. It's just that we are all so inclined to think that our own writing is clear, that if our readers struggle to understand it, then the problem must be not our flawed expression but their shallow reading.

But that's a mistake, because if we underestimate our readers' real needs, we risk losing more than their attention. We risk

losing what writers since Aristotle have called a reliable *ethos*—
the character that readers infer from our writing: does our writing make them think we are difficult or accessible? trustworthy
or deceitful? amiably candid or impersonally aloof?

Over time, the ethos we project in individual pieces of writing hardens into our reputation. So it's not just altruistically gen-
erous to go an extra step to help readers. It's pragmatically smart,
because we tend to trust most a writer with a reputation for being thoughtful, reliable, and considerate of her readers' needs.

But what is at stake here is not just reputation, but the ethical foundations of a literate society. We write ethically when, as
a matter of principle, we would trade places with our intended
readers and experience the consequences they do after they
read our writing. Unfortunately, it's not quite that simple. How,
for example, do we think about those who write opaquely without knowing they do; or those who knowingly write that way
and defend it?

Unintended Obscurity

Those who write in ways that seem dense and convoluted rarely
think they do. For example, I do not believe that the writers of
this next passage *knowingly* wrote it as unclearly as they did:

> A major condition affecting adult reliance on early communicative
> patterns is the extent to which the communication has been
> planned prior to its delivery. Adult speech behaviour takes on
> many of the characteristics of child language, where the commu-
> nication is spontaneous and relatively unpredictable.

> —E. Ochs and B. Schieffelin,
> *Planned and Unplanned Discourse*

That means (I think),

> When we speak spontaneously, we rely on patterns of child
> language.

The authors might object that I have oversimplified their idea,
but those eleven words express what I remember from their

forty-four, and what really counts, after all, is not what we understand *as* we read, but how clearly we remember it.

The ethical issue here is not those writers' willful indifference, but their innocent ignorance. In that case, when writers don't know better, readers have the duty to meet another term of the reader-writer contract: we must not just read carefully, but when given the opportunity, respond candidly and helpfully. I know many of you think that right now you do not have the standing to do that. But one day, you will.

Intended Misdirection

The ethics of writing are clearer when writers knowingly use language not to further their readers' interests but to disguise their own.

Example #1: Who Erred? a few years ago, the Sears Company was accused of overcharging for automobile repairs. It responded with an ad saying,

> With over two million automotive customers serviced last year in California alone, mistakes may have occurred. However, Sears wants you to know that we would never intentionally violate the trust customers have shown in our company for 105 years.

In the first sentence, the writer avoided mentioning Sears as the party responsible for mistakes. He could have used a passive verb:

> . . . mistakes **may have been made.**

But that would have encouraged us to wonder *By whom?* Instead, the writer found a verb that moved Sears off stage by saying mistakes just "occurred," seemingly on their own.

In the second sentence of that ad, though, the writer focused on *Sears*, the responsible agent, because he wanted to emphasize its good intentions.

> **Sears** . . . would never intentionally violate . . .

If we revise the first sentence to focus on Sears and the second to hide it, we get a different effect:

> When we serviced over two million automotive customers last year in California, we made mistakes. However, you should know that no intentional violation of 105 years of trust occurred.

That's a small point of stylistic manipulation, self-interested but innocent of any malign motives. This next one is more significant.

Example #2: Who Pays?   Consider this letter from a natural gas utility telling me and hundreds of thousands of other customers that it was raising our rates. (The topic/subject in every clause, main or subordinate, is boldfaced.)

> **The Illinois Commerce Commission** has authorized a restructuring of our rates together with an increase in Service Charge revenues effective with service rendered on and after November 12, 1990. **This** is the first increase in rates for Peoples Gas in over six years. **The restructuring of rates** is consistent with the policy of the Public Utilities Act that **rates for service to various classes of utility customers** be based upon the cost of providing that service. **The new rates** move revenues from every class of customer closer to the cost actually incurred to provide gas service.

That notice is a model of misdirection: after the first sentence, the writer never begins another with a human character, least of all the character whose interests are most at stake—me, the reader. He (or perhaps she) mentions me only twice, in the third person, never as a topic/agent/subject:

> . . . for service to various classes of utility **customers**
> . . . move revenues from every class of **customer**

The writer mentions the company only once, in the third person, and not as a responsible topic/agent/subject:

> . . . increase in rates for **Peoples Gas**

Had the company wanted to make clear who the real "doer" was and who was being done to, the notice would have read more like this:

> According to the Illinois Commerce Commission, **we** can now charge **you** more for your gas service after November 12, 1990. **We** have not made **you** pay more in over six years, but under the Public Utilities Act, now **we** can.

If the writer *intended* to deflect responsibility, then we can reasonably charge him with breaching the First Rule of Ethical Writing, for surely, he would not want that same kind of writing directed to him, systematically hiding who is doing what in a matter close to his interests.

Example #3: Who Dies?   Finally, here is a passage that raises an even greater ethical issue, one involving life and death. Some time ago, the Government Accounting Office investigated why more than half the car owners who got recall letters did not comply with them. It found that car owners could not understand the letters or were not sufficiently alarmed by them to take their cars to the dealer for service.

I received the following. It shows how writers can meet a legal obligation while evading an ethical one (I number the sentences):

> [1]A defect which involves the possible failure of a frame support plate may exist on your vehicle. [2]This plate (front suspension pivot bar support plate) connects a portion of the front suspension to the vehicle frame, and [3]its failure could affect vehicle directional control, particularly during heavy brake application. [4]In addition, your vehicle may require adjustment service to the hood secondary catch system. [5]The secondary catch may be misaligned so that the hood may not be adequately restrained to prevent hood fly-up in the event the primary latch is inadvertently left unengaged. [6]Sudden hood fly-up beyond the secondary catch while driving could impair driver visibility. [7]In certain circumstances, occurrence of either of the above conditions could result in vehicle crash without prior warning.

(When asked my make of car, I dodge the question.)
    First, look at the subject/topics of the sentences:

[1]a defect	[2]this plate	[3]its failure
[4]your vehicle	[5]the secondary catch	
[6]sudden hood fly-up	[7]occurrence of either condition	

The main character/topic of that story is not me, the driver, but
my car and its parts. In fact, the writers ignored me almost entirely (I am in *your vehicle* twice and *driver* once), and completely
removed themselves. In sum, it says,

> A car might have defective parts. Its plate could fail and its hood
> fly up. If they do, it could crash without warning.

The writers—probably a committee of lawyers—also nominal-
ized verbs and made others passive when they referred to actions
that might alarm me (n = nominalization, p = passive):

failure $_n$	vehicle directional control $_n$	heavy brake application $_n$
be misaligned $_p$	not restrained $_p$	hood fly-up $_n$
left unengaged $_p$	driver visibility $_n$	warning $_n$

If the writers intended to deflect my fear and anger at them,
then they violated their ethical duty to write to me as they would
have me write to them, for surely they would not swap places
with a reader deliberately lulled into ignoring a condition that
threatened his life.
    Of course, being candid has its costs. I would be naive to
claim that everyone is free to write as he or she pleases, especially
when a job depends on protecting an employer's self-interest.
Maybe the writers of that letter felt coerced into writing it as they
did. But that doesn't mitigate the consequences. When we knowingly write in ways that we would not want others to write to us,
we abrade the trust that sustains a civil society.
    We should not, of course, confuse unethical indirectness
with the human impulse to soften bad news. When a supervisor

says *I'm afraid our new funding didn't come through,* we know it means 'You have no job.' But that indirectness is motivated not by dishonesty, but by kindness.

In short, our choice of subjects is crucial not only when we want to be clear, but also when we want to be honest or deceptive.

RATIONALIZING OPACITY

Necessary Complexity

A more complicated ethical issue is how we should respond to those who know they write in a complex style, but claim they must, because they are breaking new intellectual ground. Are they right, or is that self-serving rationalization? This is a vexing question, not just because we can settle it only case-by-case, but because we may not be able to settle some cases at all, at least not to everyone's satisfaction.

Here, for example, is a sentence from a leading figure in contemporary literary theory:

> If, for a while, the ruse of desire is calculable for the uses of discipline soon the repetition of guilt, justification, pseudo-scientific theories, superstition, spurious authorities and classifications can be seen as the desperate effort to "normalize" *formally* the disturbance of a discourse of splitting that violates the rational, enlightened claims of its enunciatory modality.
>
> —Homi K. Babba

Does that sentence express a thought so complex, so nuanced that its substance can be expressed only as written? Or is it academic babble? How do we decide whether in fact his nuances are, at least for ordinarily competent readers, just not accessible, given the time most of us have to figure them out?

We owe readers an ethical duty to write precise and nuanced prose, but we ought not assume that they owe us an indefinite amount of their time to unpack it. If we choose to write in ways that we know will make readers struggle—well, it's a free country. In the marketplace of ideas, truth is the prime value, but not the only one. Another is the time it takes to find it.

In the final analysis, I can suggest only that when writers claim their prose style must be difficult because their ideas are new, they are, as a matter of simple fact, more often wrong than right. The philosopher of language Ludwig Wittgenstein said,

> Whatever can be thought can be thought clearly; whatever can be written can be written clearly.

I'd add a nuance:

> . . . and with just a bit more effort, more clearly.

Salutary Complexity/Subversive Clarity

There are two more defenses of complexity: one claims that complexity is good for us, the other that clarity is bad.

As to the first claim, some argue that the harder we have to work to understand what we read, the more deeply we think and the better we understand. Everyone should be happy to know that no evidence supports so foolish a claim, and substantial evidence contradicts it.

As to the second claim, some argue that "clarity" is a device wielded by those in power to mislead us about who really controls our lives. By speaking and writing in deceptively simple ways, they say, those who control the facts dumb them down, rendering us unable to understand the truth about our political and social circumstances:

> The call to write curriculum in a language that is touted as clear and accessible is evidence of a moral and political vision that increasingly collapses under the weight of its own anti-intellectualism. . . . [T]hose who make a call for clear writing synonymous with an attack on critical educators have missed the role that the "language of clarity" plays in a dominant culture that cleverly and powerfully uses "clear" and "simplistic" language to systematically undermine and prevent the conditions from arising for a public culture to engage in rudimentary forms of complex and critical thinking.
>
> —Stanley Aronowitz, *Postmodern Education*

The writer makes one good point: language is deeply implicated in politics, ideology, and control. In our earliest history, the educated elite used writing itself to exclude the illiterate, then Latin and French to exclude those who knew only English. More recently, those in authority have relied on a vocabulary thick with Latinate nominalizations and on a Standard English that requires those Outs aspiring to join the Ins to submit to a decade-long education, during which time they are expected to acquire not only the language of the Ins, but their values, as well.

Moreover, clarity is not a natural virtue, corrupted by fallen academics, bureaucrats, and others jealous to preserve their illegitimate authority. Clarity is a value that is created by society and that society must work hard to maintain, for it is not just hard to write clearly. It is almost an unnatural act. It has to be learned, sometimes painfully (as this book demonstrates).

So is clarity an ideological value? Well of course it is. How could it not be?

But those who attack clarity as a conspiracy to oversimplify complicated social issues are as wrong as those who attack science because some use it for malign ends: neither science nor clarity is a threat; we are threatened by those who use clarity (or science) to deceive us. It is not clarity that subverts, but the unethical use of it. We must simply insist that, in principle, those who manage our affairs have a duty to tell us the truth as clearly as they can. They probably won't, but that just shifts the burden to us to call them out on it.

With every sentence we write we have to choose, and the ethical quality of our choices depends on the motives behind them. Only by knowing motives can we know whether a writer of clear or complex prose would willingly be the object of such writing, to be influenced (or manipulated) in the same way, with the same result.

That seems simple enough. But it's not.

An Extended Analysis

It is easy to abuse writers who seem to manipulate us through their language for their own, self-interested ends. It is more difficult to think about these matters when we are manipulated by the language of those whom we would never charge with deceit. But it is just such cases that force us to think hard about matters of style and ethics.

The most celebrated texts in our history are the Declaration of Independence, the Constitution, and Abraham Lincoln's Gettysburg Address and Second Inaugural Address. In previous editions of this book, I discussed how Lincoln artfully manipulated the language in both his speeches. Here I examine how Thomas Jefferson managed his prose style in our Declaration of Independence to influence how we respond to his argument.

The Declaration is celebrated for its logic. After a discussion of human rights and their origin, Jefferson laid out a simple syllogism:

> **Major premise:**   When a long train of abuses by a government evinces a design to reduce a people under despotism, they must throw off such government.
>
> **Minor Premise:**   These colonies have been abused by a tyrant who evinces such a design.
>
> **Conclusion:**   We therefore throw off that government and declare that these colonies are free and independent states.

Jefferson's argument is as straightforward as the language expressing it is artful.

Jefferson begins with a preamble that explains why the colonists decided to explain their declaration:

> When, in the course of human events, it becomes necessary for one people to dissolve the political bonds which have connected them with another, and to assume among the powers of the earth, the separate and equal station to which the laws of nature and of nature's God entitle them, a decent respect to the opinions of mankind requires that they should declare the causes which impel them to the separation.

He then organizes the Declaration into three parts. In the first, he offers as his major premise, a philosophical justification for a people to throw off a tyranny and replace it with a government of their own:

> We hold these truths to be self-evident, that all men are created equal, that they are endowed by their Creator with certain unalienable rights, that among these are life, liberty and the pursuit of happiness. That to secure these rights, governments are instituted among men, deriving their just powers from the consent of the governed. That whenever any form of government becomes destructive to these ends, it is the right of the people to alter or to abolish it, and to institute new government, laying its foundation on such principles and organizing its powers in such form, as to them shall seem most likely to effect their safety and happiness. Prudence, indeed, will dictate that governments long established should not be changed for light and transient causes; and accordingly all experience hath shown that mankind are more disposed to suffer, while evils are sufferable, than to right themselves by abolishing the forms to which they are accustomed. But when a long train of abuses and usurpations, pursuing invariably the same object evinces a design to reduce them under absolute despotism, it is their right, it is their duty, to throw off such government, and to provide new guards for their future security.

In Part 2, Jefferson applies these principles to the colonists' situation:

> Such has been the patient sufferance of these colonies; and such is now the necessity which constrains them to alter their former systems of government. The history of the present King of Great Britain is a history of repeated injuries and usurpations, all having in direct object the establishment of an absolute tyranny over these states. To prove this, let facts be submitted to a candid world.

Those facts constitute a list of King George's offenses against the colonies, evidence supporting Jefferson's minor premise that the king intended to establish "an absolute Tyranny over these States":

> He has refused his assent to laws, the most wholesome and necessary for the public good.
>
> He has forbidden his governors to pass laws of immediate and pressing importance . . .
>
> He has refused to pass other laws for the accommodation of large districts of people . . .

> He has called together legislative bodies at places unusual, uncomfortable, and distant . . .

Part 3 opens by reviewing the colonists' attempts to avoid separation:

> In every stage of these oppressions we have petitioned for redress in the most humble terms: Our repeated petitions have been answered only by repeated injury. A prince, whose character is thus marked by every act which may define a tyrant, is unfit to be the ruler of a free people.
>
> Nor have we been wanting in attention to our British brethren. We have warned them from time to time of attempts by their legislature to extend an unwarrantable jurisdiction over us. We have reminded them of the circumstances of our emigration and settlement here. We have appealed to their native justice and magnanimity, and we have conjured them by the ties of our common kindred to disavow these usurpations, which would inevitably interrupt our connections and correspondence. We must, therefore, acquiesce in the necessity, which denounces our separation, and hold them, as we hold the rest of mankind, enemies in war, in peace friends.

Part 3 ends with the actual declaration of independence:

> We, therefore, the representatives of the United States of America, in General Congress, assembled, appealing to the Supreme Judge of the world for the rectitude of our intentions, do, in the name, and by the authority of the good people of these colonies, solemnly publish and declare, that these united colonies are, and of right ought to be free and independent states; that they are absolved from all allegiance to the British Crown, and that all political connection between them and the state of Great Britain, is and ought to be totally dissolved; and that as free and independent states, they have full power to levy war, conclude peace, contract alliances, establish commerce, and to do all other acts and things which independent states may of right do. And for the support of this declaration, with a firm reliance on the protection of divine providence, we mutually pledge to each other our lives, our fortunes and our sacred honor.

Jefferson's argument is a model of cool logic, but as logical as it is, he artfully managed his language in its tacit support.

Parts 2 and 3 reflect the principles of clarity explained in Lessons 3–7. In part 2, Jefferson made *He* (King George) the short, concrete topic/subject/agent of all the actions named.

He *has refused* . . .

He *has forbidden* . . .

He *has refused* . . .

He *has called together* . . .

He could have written this:

His assent to laws, the most wholesome and necessary for the public good, *has not been forthcoming* . . .

Laws of immediate and pressing importance *have been forbidden* . . .

Places unusual, uncomfortable, and distant from the depository of public records *have been required* as meeting places of legislative bodies . . .

Or he could have consistently focused on the colonists:

We *have been deprived* of laws, the most wholesome and necessary . . .

We *lack* laws of immediate and pressing importance . . .

We *have had to meet* at places unusual, uncomfortable . . .

In other words, Jefferson was not forced by the nature of things to make King George the willfully active agent of every abuse. But that choice supported his argument that the king was an abusive tyrant. Such a choice seems so natural, however, that we don't notice it was a *choice*.

In Part 3, Jefferson also wrote in a style that reflects our principles of clarity: he again matched the characters in his story to the subject/topics of his sentences and used verbs to express their crucial actions. But here he switched characters to the colonists, named *we:*

Nor *have* **we** *been wanting* in attentions to our British brethren.

We *have warned* them from time to time . . .

We *have reminded* them of the circumstances of our emigration . . .

> **We** *have appealed* to their native justice and magnanimity . . .
>
> . . . **we** *have conjured* them by the ties of our common kindred . . .
>
> **They** too *have been deaf* to the voice of justice and of consanguinity.
>
> **We** *must,* therefore, *acquiesce* in the necessity . . .
>
> **We** . . . *do* . . . solemnly *publish and declare* . . .
>
> . . . **we** mutually *pledge* to each other our Lives . . .

With the one exception of *They too have been deaf,* all the subject/topics are *we.*

And again, Jefferson was not forced by the nature of things to do that. He could have made his British brethren subject/topics:

> **Our British brethren** *have heard* our requests . . .
>
> **They** *have received* our warnings . . .
>
> **They** *know* the circumstances of our emigration . . .
>
> **They** *have ignored* our pleas . . .

But he chose to assign agency to the colonists to focus readers on their attempts to negotiate, then on their action of declaring independence.

Again, his choices seem natural, even unremarkable, but they were not inevitable. What more is there to say about the style of parts 2 and 3, other than that Jefferson made the obviously right choices?

Far more interesting are Jefferson's choices in part 1, the words we have committed to our national memory. But in that part, he chose a style quite different. In fact, in part 1, he wrote only two sentences that make a real person the subject of an active verb naming an action that person performs:

> . . . **they** [the colonists] *should declare* the causes . . .
>
> **We** *hold* these truths to be self-evident . . .

There are four other subject-verb sequences that have short, concrete subjects, but they are all in the passive voice:

> . . . **all men** *are created* equal . . .

> . . . **they** *are endowed* by their Creator with certain unalienable rights . . .
>
> . . . **governments** *are instituted* among men . . .
>
> . . . **governments long established** *should* not *be changed* for light and transient causes . . .

The agency in the first two sentences is obviously God, but the last two passives explicitly obscure the agency of people in general and the colonists in particular.

In the rest of part 1, Jefferson chose a style that is *even more* impersonal, making abstractions the topic/subject/agents of almost every important verb. In fact, most of his sentences would yield to the kind of revisions we described in Lessons 2–6:

> When in the course of human events, **it** *becomes necessary* for one people to dissolve the political bands which have connected them with another . . .

> ✓ When in the course of human events, **we** *decide* **we** *should dissolve* the political bands which have . . .

> . . . **a decent respect to the opinions of mankind** *requires* that they should declare **the causes** which *impel* them to the separation.

> ✓ If **we** decently *respect* the opinions of mankind, **we** *will declare* why **we** *have decided to separate.*

> . . . **it** *is the right* of the people to alter or to abolish it, and to institute new government . . .

> ✓ **We** *may exercise* our right to *alter or abolish* it, and *institute* new government . . .

> **Prudence,** indeed, *will dictate* that governments long established should not be changed for light and transient causes . . .

> ✓ If **we** *are prudent*, **we** *will not change* governments long established for light and transient causes.

> . . . **all experience** *hath shewn*, that **mankind** *are more disposed* to suffer, while evils are sufferable . . .

> ✓ **We** *know* from experience that **we** can *choose* to *suffer* those evils that are sufferable . . .

. . . **a long train of abuses and usurpations** . . . *evinces* a design to reduce them under absolute despotism.

✓ **We** *can see* a design in a long train of abuses and usurpations pursuing invariably the same object—to reduce us under absolute despotism.

Necessity . . . *constrains* them to alter their former systems of government.

✓ **We** now *must alter* our former systems of government.

Instead of writing as clearly and directly as he did in parts 2 and 3, why in part 1 did Jefferson *choose* to write in a style so indirect and impersonal? One ready answer is that he wanted to lay down a philosophical basis not to justify our revolution in particular, but just revolutions in general, a profoundly destabilizing idea in Western political philosophy and one that needed more justification than the colonists' mere desire to throw off a government they disliked.

But what is most striking about the style of part 1 is not just its impersonal generality, but how relentlessly Jefferson uses that style to strip the colonists of any free will and to invest agency in higher forces that *coerce* the colonists to act:

- **respect** for opinion *requires* that [the colonists] explain their action
- **causes** *impel* [the colonists] to separate
- **prudence** *dictates* that [the colonists] not change government lightly
- **experience** has *shown* [the colonists]
- **necessity** *constrains* [the colonists]

Jefferson echoes that coercive power over the colonists in part 3:

- **We** *must . . . acquiesce [to] the necessity,* which denounces our separation.

Even when abstractions do not explicitly coerce the colonists, Jefferson implies that they are not free agents:

- It [is] *necessary* to sever bonds.
- Mankind *are disposed* to suffer.
- It is their *duty* to throw off a tyrant.

In this light, even *We hold these truth to be self-evident* is a claim that implies that the colonists did not discover those truths, but rather, those truths imposed themselves on the colonists.

In short, Jefferson manipulated his language three times, twice in ways that seem transparent, unremarkable, so predictable that we don't even notice the choice: in part 2, he made King George a freely acting agent of his actions by making him the subject/topic of every sentence; in part 3, Jefferson made the colonists the agents of their own actions.

But to make the first part of his argument work, Jefferson had to make the colonists seem to be the coerced objects of higher powers. Since the only higher power named in the Declaration is a Creator, nature's God, that Creator is impliedly the coercive power that "constrains them to alter their former systems of government." But he did not explicitly *say* that, much less defend it. Instead, he let the grammar of his sentences make that part of his argument for him.

The Declaration of Independence is a majestic document for reasons beyond its style and argument. The same words that freed us from tyranny laid down the fundamental values that justify the self-governance of all people everywhere.

But we ought not ignore Jefferson's rhetorical powers, and in particular, the genius of his style. He created a relentlessly logical argument justifying our independence, but he also manipulated, managed, massaged—call it what you will—spun his language to support his logic in ways not apparent to a casual reading.

If his end did not justify his means, we might argue that Jefferson was being deceptive here, using language instead of argument to establish the crucial premise to his argument: the colonists were not free to do other than what they did; they had no choice but to revolt.

It is, finally, an ethical issue. Do we trust a writer who seeks to manage our responses not just explicitly with a logical argument but implicitly through his prose style? We would say *No* about the writer of that automobile recall letter, because it was almost certainly *intended* to deceive us. We are, however, likely to say *Yes* about Jefferson, but only if we agree that his intended end justified his means, a principle that we ordinarily reject on ethical grounds.

SUMMING UP

How, finally, do we decide what counts as "good" writing? Is it clear, graceful, and candid, even if it fails to achieve its end? Or is it writing that does a job, regardless of its integrity and means? We have a problem so long as *good* can mean either ethically sound or pragmatically successful.

We resolve that dilemma by our First Principle of Ethical Writing:

> We are ethical writers when we would willingly put ourselves in the place of our readers and experience what they do as they read what we've written.

That puts the burden on us to imagine our readers and their feelings.

If you are even moderately advanced in your academic or professional career, you've experienced the consequences of unclear writing, especially when it's your own. If you are in your early years of college, though, you may wonder whether all this talk about clarity, ethics, and ethos is just so much finger wagging. At the moment, you may be happy to find enough words to fill three pages, much less worry about their clarity. And you may be reading textbooks that have been heavily edited to make them clear to first-year students who know little or nothing about their content. So you may not yet have experienced much carelessly dense writing. But it's only a matter of time before you will.

Others wonder why they should struggle to learn to write clearly when bad writing seems so common and costs its writers so little. What experienced readers know, and you eventually will, is that clear and graceful writers are so few that when we find them, we are desperately grateful. They do not go unrewarded.

I also know that for many writers the pleasure of crafting a good sentence or paragraph is often just in the achievement of it. It is an ethical satisfaction some of us find not just in writing, but in everything we do: we take pleasure in doing good work, no matter the job, no matter whether others notice. It is a view expressed by the philosopher Alfred North Whitehead, with both clarity and grace (my emphasis in the last sentence):

> Finally, there should grow the most austere of all mental qualities; I mean the sense for style. It is an aesthetic sense, based on admiration for the direct attainment of a foreseen end, simply and without waste. Style in art, style in literature, style in science, style in logic, style in practical execution have fundamentally the same aesthetic qualities, namely, attainment and restraint. The love of a subject in itself and for itself, where it is not the sleepy pleasure of pacing a mental quarter-deck, is the love of style as manifested in that study. Here we are brought back to the position from which we started, the utility of education. Style, in its finest sense, is the last acquirement of the educated mind; it is also the most useful. It pervades the whole being. The administrator with a sense for style hates waste; the engineer with a sense for style economizes his material; the artisan with a sense for style prefers good work. *Style is the ultimate morality of mind.*
>
> —Alfred North Whitehead, *The Aims of Education and Other Essays*

Index